THE HIGH
LONESOME

Epic Solo Climbing Stories

THE HIGH
LONESOME

Epic Solo Climbing Stories

EDITED BY JOHN LONG
AND
HAI-VAN K. SPONHOLZ

FALCON®

HELENA, MONTANA

A FALCON GUIDE®

Falcon® Publishing is continually expanding its list of recreational guidebooks. All books include detailed descriptions, accurate maps, and all information necessary for enjoyable trips. You can order extra copies of this book and get information and prices for other Falcon books by writing Falcon, P.O. Box 1718, Helena, MT 59624 or calling toll free 1-800-582-2665. Also, please ask for a free copy of our current catalog. Visit our website at www.FalconOutdoors.com or contact us by e-mail at falcon@falcon.com

Printed in Canada.

1 2 3 4 5 6 7 8 9 0 TP 04 03 02 01 00 99

All design and prepress work by Falcon® Publishing, Inc., Helena, Montana.

Grateful acknowledgment is made to those who granted permission to reprint the selections in this book. A complete list of copyright permissions can be found on page 164.

Library of Congress Cataloging-in-Publication Data

The high lonesome : epic solo climbing stories / edited by John Long.
        p. cm.
    ISBN 1-56044-858-X (pbk.)
    1. Mountaineers Biography. 2. Mountaineering. I. Long, John,
    1953-   . II. Title: Epic solo climbing stories.
    GV199.9.H55 1999
    796.52'2'0922–dc21
    [B]
                                                                99-28159
                                                                CIP

Project Editor: John Burbidge
Production Editor: Larissa Berry
Copyeditor: Durrae Johanek
Page Compositor: Laura Ottoson
Book design by Jeff Wincapaw
Cover design by Matt Brunt

CAUTION

Outdoor recreational activities are by their very nature potentially hazardous. All participants in such activities must assume responsibility for their own actions and safety. The information contained in this book cannot replace sound judgment and good decision-making skills, which help reduce risk exposure, nor does the scope of this book allow for disclosure of all the potential hazards and risks involved in such activities.

Learn as much as possible about the outdoor recreational activities in which you participate, prepare for the unexpected, and be cautious. The reward will be a safer and more enjoyable experience.

CONTENTS

He's got a rope, but he's not using it. Dean Potter speed-soloing the 2,000-foot-high face of Half Dome in Yosemite, 1999. PHOTO BY HEINZ ZAK

INTRODUCTION

The soloist climbs alone. He is the Lone Rider of Cowboy lore, the Wandering Jew and Moses on High. We marvel at his nerve, his personal covenant with earth and elements, his technical wizardry. And we wonder about his seeming autonomy from the shackles of society. Up on the High Lonesome, the soloist answers to his own standards, the climbing at hand and God, in that order.

Scrambling unroped over easy terrain is a required part of climbing, particularly in the mountains, where alpinists use speed to outclimb storms. Top rock climbers also enjoy "free soloing" (sans rope and protective gear) well within their abilities, with nothing but their mind for a backup. But what of rock climbers who free solo damn near the hardest routes, or mountaineers who tackle the biggest and nastiest peaks all by their lonesome?

There is the macho element. As Hemingway said of bullfighting, it takes more *cajones* to be a sportsman when death is a closer party to the game. But extreme soloing requires so much focus, precision and control that, whereas machismo might initially spur a soloist, only superior technique and mental steel can see him through. Accordingly, soloing evokes feelings of mastery and command, plus a raw intensity that even a million-dollar-a-year ballplayer can never experience. And therein lies the snare. Following a particularly rewarding solo, when everything has clicked, the climber feels like a magician. Such feelings can foster delusions of invincibility. So it's not unheard of that a narrow escape is followed by an eagerness to push things just a tiny bit further, for desire is the sequel to danger. Soon the soloist is courting doom, and he'll quickly find it if he doesn't back off. The whole insidious business is closely tied to anything that is exhilarating, deadly and fiendishly addictive. The trick is knowing when to stop or back off (providing you can), a fact lost on several of the climbers in the following stories—and each one paid for it

1

Mark Twight soloing mixed ice, rock and snow on Mont Blanc du Tacul in the Alps.
PHOTO BY ACE KVALE/TWIGHT COLLECTION.

with their life. While the rewards are great, no practice is less forgiving. On solos of any real length, if you fall, you almost certainly die.

The stories in this collection showcase climbers who were courting many things—new frontiers, impossible challenges, technical limits, self-discovery, the unknown. But no matter what reasons solo climbers may give, each is courting doom. The dangers are real and palpable and hover over every line in every story to create a vortex that sucks us, body and soul, onto the rock wall or mountain of ice. All great adventure stories make readers experience the event by proxy; solo-climbing stories are especially effective in accomplishing this. Perhaps best of all, to get the full wallop, a reader needs to know no more about climbing than one would about sailing to appreciate seafaring epics.

The following accounts vary from the little known to the historic. The focus is on stories, but several profiles and essays allow us to appreciate soloing in a more thorough way, and help untangle the controversies that are tied to several of the most famous climbs. Nevertheless, the bulk of these accounts are first-person, meaning we get the business "neat," with no intermediary author interpreting the experience on our behalf. Brief introductory passages provide some little context for the stories, but I trust the stories to tell themselves. I am not alone is believing that solo climbing stories are a unique medium in the field of adventure writing. They are a blast to read. They cast our imaginations into situations that make us rethink the meaning of what we're doing with our lives—or *not* doing. Many sages have said that a creative life requires risk. Welcome to the arena where men and women have risked all. It is up to each reader to discover why.

THE SHROUD SOLO

by Ivan Ghirardini

*C*risis can show us thoughts and feelings we otherwise have no access to, enmeshed as we are with our habitual ways of living. Sometimes the insights are subtle. And sometimes, if our crisis runs to Homeric proportions, we have a spiritual experience that repaginates our entire system, bottom to top. That Ivan Ghirardini should experience such an awakening is rare enough; that the experience would fundamentally be self-induced and would take place in the mid-1970s during the first solo winter ascent of The Shroud, one of the French Alps' grimmest testpieces, is unique. Since Ghirardini short-hands all technical descriptions, the casual reader has no way of knowing that the Frenchman tackled a 5,000-foot sheet of steep, occasionally overhanging glare ice, with momentary escape available only on wee niches in the flanking rock walls, and where the only way off was up. And surmounting the near mile-long ice chute does not ensure success, as the plateau above is often a maelstrom of wind, driving snow and lightning (following an early ascent, Yosemite legend and pioneer Frank Sachar died on this very plateau). Obvious enough, however, are the stark realizations that came to the 21-year-old alpinist while recuperating in a French hospital bed.

‡   ‡   ‡

The nurse's scissors freed me from my winding sheet—my clothes frozen stiff as a board on the outside and damp and clay-cold on my numbed body. It was with a feeling of faint surprise that I watched my body emerge, emaciated, bruised by its days in the storm, without food or drink. My hands and feet were purple and blue, swollen with frostbite; already on my toes were telltale black blotches. I lay with my eyes half-closed.

4

Through the thick, stifling mists around me, I caught snatches of conversation: "Heartbeat's a bit irregular. Ah, that's better. Body temperature's rising now, too. My God, his blood's so thick I can't even get a blood sample!" But I felt quite indifferent, unconcerned, unmoved.

Soon the drips were in place, the instruments set up. As I lay quietly, in those warm, dry sheets, my shivers stilled; my knotted muscles relaxed; my very bones seemed to settle into their normal stations. And yet I was unable to shake off a feeling of utter despair. Here I was, back in the world of men, surrounded by kindness, nursed devotedly, and yet I felt myself alone, most horribly alone.

Days passed. Lying on my hospital bed, I felt drained, finished, infinitely old despite my 21 years. I had had many visitors; plenty of people had been eager to see the young man who had dared, alone and in winter, to brave *The Shroud* on the north face of the Grandes Jorasses. I had been deeply touched by the instinctive solidarity so many had shown. But had they understood? If so, how could they still speak of "exploit," of "uncommon physical resistance," of "courage," "will" and "daring"? None of these qualities were mine. No credit was due to me for having succeeded in my ascent, and it would have been vain of me to pretend otherwise. In going beyond my limits I had broken every law of nature, had endangered not only my own life, but others. And yet one thing I could claim. There on the mountain I had lived for a few days the life of the visionary, the mystic, prey to a spiritual exaltation undreamed of before. Thus I had no regrets, no regrets even for the horrors of the descent. The intensity of the experience I had lived was above and beyond anything I had previously known.

At first sight there was nothing to orient me toward an alpine and guiding career. Indeed I had discovered the Alpine world only by accident through a book by Walter Bonatti. I had been fascinated by his account of his ascent of the Petit Dru. Fired by a spirit of emulation, I decided to become a guide, and to the distress of my parents, modest Italian immigrants, I gave up my studies.

Alone and untutored, I acquired rock and ice-climbing techniques, learning painfully from my own mistakes. I improved rapidly—perhaps too rapidly, becoming overconfident, cocksure. So perfectly at home did I feel on medium-standard rock that I undertook a series of long solo climbs for which in all probability I was not sufficiently competent.

My audacity paid off, however, and I felt myself somehow protected. My greatest happiness lay always in my solitary bivouacs, on the summit of some great peak after a difficult and successful climb. My finest memories are of days spent cowering on some great face in the teeth of the storm. It was then that I felt myself to be living in a sort of limbo that was no longer the world of the living but not yet the world of the dead. Many dismissed me as a tearaway, rash, sick or even deranged.

I find it difficult to isolate the factors that drove me to such tests, but one thing I feel is clear: my acts were only rarely willed by myself alone, only rarely freely undertaken. I felt myself something other, a plaything of impulses and inner compulsions that I did not control. I simply let myself be led, knowing that all was inevitable and that to oppose my will to this mysterious imperative would be an act not of self-assertion but of obstruction. Climbing solo taught me to control my thoughts, to discipline my fears, to debate with myself, in short was a process of self-education.

It was thus that I came to find my own mediocrity and that of the world around me intolerable. I recognized that I, like most of the other inhabitants of my planet, was degenerate. I was only 21, yet I possessed not a single one of my own teeth, and was sick after virtually every meal. I realized that I was not a man in the full sense of the word, not worthy to be called "man," and the realization was so bitter that often I wept. We forget that we have the potential to be children of God, to be men in Christ's image.

If I undertook *The Shroud*, it was precisely for that reason: to submit myself and my life to God's purpose. No longer could I tolerate my own mediocrity, no longer tolerate the unmistakable signs of my own degeneracy, physical and mental. And it was, of course, a wholly egotistic act.

What I planned was entirely beyond my capability. I intended to follow the first third of the *Desmaison Route* on the Walker Spur, traverse out onto *The Shroud* above the gullies, and then climb direct to the summit over the wall where Serge Gousseault had met his death. I had determined to start my ascent on Sunday, February 23, come what may; I had an inner conviction that the weather would be good.

I had no down clothing and the rock was covered with verglas, and yet I felt no cold in my hands as I climbed the first 1,200 feet of the *Direct Route*. So heavy was my rucksack that I had to do each pitch twice; I had had to bring a large quantity of equipment to enable me to climb the overhanging walls that would confront me toward the summit of the route. At night, however, hanging from tape-slings on pegs (I had no ice-screws), I shivered, poorly protected by my little bivouac tent. Luckily, I had the comfort brought by hot drinks.

The first four days were without incident; it would be pedantry to describe them. As I moved higher up the face, I lost all sense of time. In that utter solitude, I forgot exhaustion, thirst, hunger, cold. On the black ice of *The Shroud*, glassy, brittle, I was unaware of danger or difficulty. Without protection I would climb long pitches, balancing on my frontpoints which bit only marginally into the ice. I would spend whole precious minutes, unknowing, studying air-bubbles trapped in the ice or admiring the colors of a little patch of lichen on the rock. There were times when I forgot I had a summit to reach, and it was only when the vertiginous steepness of the face brought me to myself that I would shake off my inactivity and move on toward the summit.

On Wednesday, February 26, I bivouacked on the rock outcrop in the center of *The Shroud*. As I was changing the gas cylinder on the stove, I dropped the valve screw. I had no option but to throw away my stove. Many other things too became useless: I threw away my spare gas cylinders, all the dried foods I had brought, my dried meat and ham which were now inedible. All that night, I broke off pieces of ice and sucked them to quench my thirst. My throat throbbed and burned, but I was not dismayed. I could so easily have retreated; some twenty abseils would have brought me safely to the foot of the face. But I was not master of my own fate; I had to go on. To lighten my load I reluctantly left some climbing equipment, including my two 120-foot ropes. I resolved to make for the Hirondelles Ridge. Every 30 feet I had to stop, exhausted, to control my breathing and ease the cramped muscles in my calves. Never had I suffered so. Any slightest mistake and I would have fallen to a certain death. Slowly, slowly, my fear grew, and as it grew, so did my exhaustion.

I was only 150 feet from the ridge when I heard a helicopter; it was the mountain rescue service. I drove a peg into the snow, belayed myself and raised my arms in a V-sign to signal my predicament; in the cabin I could see two men come to save me, and I wept. I stood there for several minutes, still as a statue, my arms raised, then I extracted my peg and went on. The helicopter clattered away; I was convinced that they would come and collect me on the ridge. My momentary breakdown had given me a new surge of strength, and it was almost at a run that I finished that last pitch. *The Shroud* was conquered; I knew, however, that I was finished too, unless I was saved.

A freezing bivouac in a hollow in the rocks was followed by an unforgettable sunrise over the Valais. After five days in the somber shadows of the north face, I felt myself warmed and comforted, in spite of the biting wind, by the sun's welcome rays. I went on, despite my exhaustion, my deadly exhaustion. I had to throw away much of my equipment, items which had been with me since the beginning of my career as a solo climber and to which I was as attached as is the craftsman to his tools. There were moments when my eyes misted over, my legs tottered and I had to stop and breathe deeply. All I had left were three biscuits and a few lumps of sugar, but I was not hungry. At about midday, I reached the point where the Tronchey and Hirondelles ridges meet. There, in front of me, was the summit; I was almost there when the helicopter appeared again. As it circled me, I made the standard distress signal. Then, inexplicably, I had the same reaction as on the previous day; I ran toward the summit. My would-be rescuers supposed I was quite well, and went away.

At the summit I collapsed on the snow, sobbing. It was no doubt a consequence of dehydration and of exhaustion. When finally I got to my feet, my head was spinning so that I nearly keeled over the cornice onto the north face. I rested for a long time, then set off down to Courmayeur. At every step I sank into the snow up to my knees; after every ten steps I stopped, and sometimes crumpled to the ground. When I reached the Rocher du Reposoir, I came to a final halt; I was too low, but I could no longer summon up the strength to fight my way back up. That evening, a red helicopter came straight toward me from the Col des Grandes Jorasses. For the third time I made the distress signal, but although they passed directly overhead, my rescuers failed to see me. On the horizon, to the west, a great wall of cloud was rising in the sky; the storm was coming.

I shall not attempt to describe the six days I spent up there at some 11,000 feet, with no food or drink, buffeted by storm and avalanche; it would be impossible. I ought to have died, but thinking of my parents' grief, I fought for life. I prayed as I had never prayed before, but with this difference, that now I felt myself in direct contact with Him to whom my prayers were addressed.

On Monday, March 6, at about 2 A.M., the helicopter came. During that night I had been assured of its coming. With exemplary courage and skill, the pilot held his machine steady over me. At any moment, the cloud might sweep across between him and me. I watched as my rescuer came slowly down to me on a steel cable. He fastened me on in his place. I felt a jerk. I was saved from death. Never will I forget those seconds.

On *The Shroud*, I was using the mountains as a refuge from a life and a reality I was too weak and cowardly to face. Now that I have come back from death, I have embarked on a long and arduous process of regeneration that will require the dedication of my entire life, as well as rigorous physical and mental self-discipline. Of what use are extreme faces? It is within that we find the most insurmountable barriers. We shall not find the seventh grade beyond the sixth, but in ourselves.

But enough of words.

THE DESIRE: A SOLO ASCENT OF THE DIHEDRAL WALL

by Jim Beyer

*I*t *is said that the loneliest person on earth is found in the still of night, dangling on the side of a big wall. Alone. Soloing big walls is a peculiar trade, difficult to rationalize from afar not only for the isolation, difficulty and dangers involved, but also for the brutal labor. A solo wall climber must ascend a pitch, rappel back down and then reclimb the pitch to clean the gear and regain the highpoint. By the time a soloist tops out he has descended the entire wall one time and climbed it twice. The following two articles, one written by Jim Beyer and the other about him, look into the singular experiences of the solo wall climber. One of the most accomplished American soloists, Beyer soloed many new wall routes throughout the continental United States, then ventured to the Karakoram and spent thirteen days soloing a 54-pitch route up Grand Cathedral (V1 5.10 A4), perhaps the greatest solo first ascent of a rock wall ever done. We start here with Beyer describing a solo ascent of El Capitan in Yosemite, one of the first of many walls that distinguished Beyer and a few others who found their calling by climbing alone on the High Lonesome.*

‡   ‡   ‡

Sometimes I'm inclined to take on projects without the assistance of even the closest friends. I like to solo, had done several walls previously in this fashion, and had a good idea of what it would take to do El Cap. A solo attempt would be a worthwhile project.

But which route? From previous experience I had developed a passionate hatred of soloing hard free climbing. In my eyes, soloing was either a beautiful experience or a bum trip; technical difficulty is not always the deciding factor. It's all about a state of mind.

The *Dihedral Wall* seemed a logical choice, with a minimum of free climbing and mostly moderate nailing. Although capable of harder things, I figured that just being on El Cap alone would be hard enough for my mind to rationalize.

I planned the climb for the spring and started to accumulate gear, but when I arrived in the Valley I didn't feel up to soloing the wall. I soloed a lesser wall instead. After a summer in the mountains, I returned to Yosemite in mid-August, determined to attempt the route. Daily 105-degree temperatures nixed that plan, but late September found me hauling my bag up the second pitch. I planned to go for it the next day.

Walking through Camp 4 at dusk, I ran into an old climbing partner and we decided to do a couple of free climbs before my departure. The next day I fell off *Wheat Thin* and fractured my heel bone on a protruding knob. After crutching around the Valley for a week or so expecting a miraculous recovery, I left, giving up hope for another attempt in 1976.

A month passed and the injury healed.

El Cap dominated my daydreams and I couldn't shake it. Soon I quit my job and started hitching to the Valley. After a proposition from one of the "boys" and a rainy night-bivouac near the interstate, I arrived.

I immediately began humping loads up to the wall. Bivouacked at the base, I thrashed in restless sleep. Would I be able to cope with the loneliness? I thought back to *The Prow* (Washington Column). After two days alone on the face I began a desperate dash for the summit, civilization and a return to sanity. Now, on El Cap, I fixed ropes over the first three pitches, then farted around for a day, lying in the meadow, gazing up at the face like a pagan worshiping the greatest idol. The route starts in a huge left-slanting dihedral; the dihedral forms the left margin of the massive high-angled slab that occupies the west end of the the face massif, a shimmering, almost flawless sheet of perfect rock.

Several hundred feet of climbing brought me to the top of the dihedral and a belay below a huge triangular roof. A bolt ladder led out right onto a big blank bulge; the bag hung free as I nailed from the end of the ladder. The next pitch led up a steep dihedral and then out onto mixed bolts, hooks and stacks. It was Thanksgiving Day, but I was content to be alone at last with more food and water than I could possibly consume. I rose with the sun and nailed a long pitch up the Black Dihedral. The last major bolt ladder headed out toward the main dihedral; the number of hangers seemed to decline the higher I got, and this pitch had only one. I stretched the lead into the 5.9 pitch without leaving my rack, doing a half-dozen aid moves. The end of the pitch proved more difficult than it looked: thrashing for several desperate minutes, I tried to defy gravity on a flake, but seventy-five pegs and eighty-five crabs felt otherwise. I reached the "The Ledge," the only bivy ledge below the twenty-first pitch, after a short rappel.

I settled in for the night, throwing empty cans of fruit and tuna off at random (to return later for them). Angry shouts floated up and I looked down at a moving blue dot at the base of my wall.

As the sun went down a wall of clouds moved up the Muir Gorge and into the Valley. Soon they blew vertically up the face and engulfed me; alert for any sign of rain, I awoke with a start, but it was only water dripping from higher up the wall. The clouds had gone, leaving a cold clear night.

I led out on the day's work: a pair of A3 pitches. It was cold, the wind blew without mercy, and I felt like a stranger in a strange land, a rock technician bashing his way up a two-dimensional world, his life-support system hauled up behind. Leading, rappelling, cleaning, hauling, racking up—it all takes a while, but finally the second pitch of the day was done. I decided to bivy again on The Ledge and was in my down gear in no time, still shivering.

Up before the sun, I climbed up my fixed ropes and started off on the next pitch, nailing out left under a roof, then up and right to a 5.0-looking off-width. The carabiner chain pulled straight out on shaky bongs as I cursed and raved until the end of the pitch. But it ended in a stance—a real treat. A man could almost stand on only one foot in an aider, instead of two.

While cleaning the last pitch of the day, the shaft of my hammer struck a wild blow on the rock. I was nailing a small, very left-slanting arch right-handed; immediately, the hammer head started to slip off—and I started to *freak!* The situation appeared critical. Climbing all that way, just to be disgraced with a rescue (maybe) only a few hundred feet from the top. I jumared the rest of the pitch, leaving a lot of pegs behind. On reaching the belay, I set up my hammock, cut a hole in a water jug and soaked the hammer overnight. After thirteen hours the wood had swollen enough to keep the head on, but after the first pitch it started to slip off again. Jesus! What now? I took the only Rurp on my rack and drove it into the shaft; it wouldn't go in all the way, but tightened things up enough to hopefully last the rest of the climb.

Two more overhanging pitches led to my fourth hammock bivy. The first few days had been relatively quiet, only the sound of the wind, clanking hardware, ringing pitons and an occasional song or curse to be heard. As the climb reached its sixth day, I realized how much I was talking to myself—in conversations, actually. I was also thinking of myself in the plural: why don't we hurry up and clean this pitch? It seemed to be a team effort.

Three mixed pitches the next day developed into the same situation that occurred the previous day: halfway up a pitch the sun went down, darkness grew. I ran out of pegs and the belay was just in sight! I reached the ledge in total darkness only to meet disappointment: it was too small to sit on, and I had left my headlamp back at the beginning of the pitch. I figured that it would be safer to free climb with no protection rather than rappel off the only fixed anchor, a single old bolt. I climbed past a fixed peg that I didn't notice till the next day and reached a ledge big enough to sit on, just thirty feet from Thanksgiving Ledge.

I climbed the remaining distance the next day, traversing Thanksgiving and fixing ropes to the third-class shoulder of El Cap. I could have slept on top that night, but instead opted to spend my eighth and final night on the wall. Flies swarmed around me as the sun set, and I reflected that until that moment I had seen neither man nor beast for eight days. Perhaps it is good to seclude oneself from mankind for short periods of time to gain some perspective.

I found an ideal bivy spot and attempted to eat all of my remaining food, watching the fire dim to smoldering coals. When I had started the wall, the moon was but a sliver. I watched it travel across the sky every night; it rose later and later as it grew and by the end was almost full.

Another warm day in the High Sierra urged me up the third- and fourth-class slabs leading to the summit of El Cap. I was relieved to find no one on top. When I solo a climb and find the summit crowded, I feel cheated. I sat down and recounted the journey day by day, content and elated—eight days alone without loneliness. And it made me wonder . . .

But the adventure wasn't over yet. Can't relax until you reach safety! One obstacle remained: how to get all that gear to the valley floor. A few hours and many rest stops later brought me to the lip of the southeast flank. I decided to ditch my gear and descend without a burden. I kicked the bag off the overhanging Zodiac Wall, trailing a partially inflated hammock as a parachute. Down the East Ledges toward safety I ran. Future climbs, future goals filtered through my mind.

PARTY OF ONE: PROFILE OF JIM BEYER, AN AMERICAN SOLOIST

by Greg Child

W*e segue to the following profile by prolific climber and writer Greg Child, in which we learn how Jim Beyer's mental and physical achievements were ultimately eclipsed by his remarkable change of heart. A legendary big wall and big mountain climber in his own right, Child appraises Beyer's many landmark solo climbs and puts them in a professional context. This helps us understand that only by stepping so far into loneliness and commitment—with only his own basic stuff to fill the void—could nature finally break Beyer's rigid code of self-reliance. Freezing and hallucinating on a wind-blasted 8,000-meter Himalayan peak, he discovers the limitations of always going it alone. On hands and knees and in defecated clothing, Jim Beyer finally finds a wormhole back to the living. In a profile as unique as the climber it features, we find how Beyer's cantankerous and unyielding spirit, which led him to such soloing heights, also led him to self-discovery and a redefining of his purpose, of his journey and of newfound desires.*

‡   ‡   ‡

I first encountered Jim Beyer from a distance, in Yosemite Valley, in 1977; he was 2,000 feet above me on El Capitan, making the first solo ascent of *The Shield*. I stood among a group of climbers in El Cap meadow, watching spring storm mists swirl around the wall. I still recall the patter of rain against our cagoules, the beat of The Grateful Dead playing from a tinny portable tape deck, and the awe that the sight of El Cap filled us with, glistening wet and gold as it did that day like a fearful, shining beast.

It was the year a druglord's plane had ditched in a frozen high-country lake, and bales of weed were still being hauled out of the ice. Life in the valley was deliciously deranged. We were young, our hair was long and we lived and breathed climbing.

The sky darkened as a Sierra thunderhead regrouped to pelt the valley with another assault of sleet. On El Cap, climbers—sodden, cold, and had-enough—could be seen rappelling off *The Nose* and *Tangerine Trip*. Only one remained—going up, not down.

"Who is that guy up there?" I asked.

"That's Jim Beyer," someone replied.

"He must be freaking out in this weather."

"Nah. Beyer can handle it. He soloed the *Dihedral Wall* last year. He likes it up there alone." I filed the name—Jim Beyer—in my memory. It would keep cropping up in years to come, attached to news of bold solos on big walls.

Clouds engulfed El Cap, and we retired to our clammy nylon abodes in Camp 4, leaving Beyer, with two-thirds of El Cap beneath him, to press on.

The headwall of *The Shield* is so overhanging—30 degrees beyond vertical—that rain doesn't touch it, but in the gloom of the storm it's cold and very, very exposed. By afternoon Beyer had nailed the crux, the Triple Cracks, anchored his rope, rappelled the pitch, and was jumaring back up and hammering out knifeblade pitons when he began inexplicably sliding down the rope. He was stung with the adrenaline shot. Something was dreadfully wrong—but what? When his jumars jammed and he jolted to a stop he looked up to see a big-wall climber's nightmare.

The sheath of his lead rope was cut through, neatly circumscribed from rubbing against a sharp burr on a piton. His weighted jumars had stripped the sheath down the rope, causing his slide, and exposing several feet of white nylon core, at which, strand by strand, the piton was sawing.

With no one but the misty sky to bitch to about it, Beyer looked up at the rope. Every movement caused the piton to cut another millimeter into the core. Later he told a friend that he begged God's help. "When nothing happened," Beyer said, "I knew there was no God."

Beyer knew he had put himself in this situation, and he alone would get himself out of it. He muscled aside fear as he jumared the fraying rope toward the belay. It was as if these adrenaline-thumping moments were meant as a test of his physical and mental training, a test to see if he really had the stomach for the life of soloing he'd mapped out for himself. The test was simple: the rope snaps, Jim dies; jumar past the fraying strands, he lives. Years later, on other walls, in other ranges, the tests would become more extreme.

This then, is the story of Jim Beyer, America's, and perhaps the world's, most accomplished big-wall soloist. It is a story of a reclusive man's 20-year solitary odyssey that's taken him quietly yet triumphantly up a score of American monoliths, and to an agonizing defeat in the Karakoram Range of Pakistan. It's a story of discovery of self through extreme climbing and, by the end, of an alchemical metamorphosis of purpose.

Who is Jim Beyer? Most readers of climbing magazines will draw a blank on the name, for he is no star of the climbing media. He doesn't pen articles about his climbs, save for understated accounts in the back pages of the *American Alpine Journal* or the one piece on his first *Dihedral Wall* solo. Never before has a photo of Beyer appeared in a magazine. He possesses neither the leonine leotards nor physique of the sport-climbing set. Beyer is a house builder, who dresses in well-worn, sawdust-scented workclothes. His Falstaffian physique is built for endurance rather than sport. He is a soloist in more avenues than climbing: he kayaks whitewater solo, and even the spec-houses he builds for a living are mostly Beyer's work alone.

Beyer is suspicious of anyone who basks in the glow of fame in climbing. Magazine profiles are anathema to him. Sponsored climbers and sport climbing heroes are "posers." Thus, it took some convincing on my part to get him to discuss his career. But talk he did, on a winter weekend in 1991 in Boulder, Colorado, in the half-finished shell of his latest house, and in Eldorado Canyon. "My agenda in spilling my guts to you," he told me, "is to show there are traditionalists left in climbing." That was his conscious agenda. If he had an unconscious agenda, then it was to unburden himself of himself, for in the world of a soloist there are few people to listen.

Beyer's brand of climbing—solo big-wall climbing—is not everyone's cup of tea. It's a slow and laborious process, a mental and physical marathon. It is, essentially, aid climbing for pitch after pitch up huge cliffs, using a roped self-belay system. Such climbs might take two weeks, and on them one must carry masses of hardware, bivouac gear, food and water. The endeavor means hauling loads weighing hundreds of pounds; it means complex rope work and sleeping in portaledges. On a hard pitch, the climber might nail fragile flakes, make multiple moves on skyhooks or step off A5 aid to begin free climbing into unknown territory—with no one at the other end of the rope to whimper to. To embark on a solo climb, the climber must be driven to succeed and fueled by a deep belief in himself. Thus, for a soloist, defeat comes hard because there is only oneself to blame for failure.

Born in Florida but a longtime resident of Colorado, Beyer made his big-wall solo debut at age 17, with *Sunshine* (V 5.9 A3) on The Diamond face of Long's Peak. The route was a first ascent—remarkable for a youngster—and it set the course of his climbing: inevitably solo, usually first ascents, unsupported and unpublicized to the extent that few people even knew where he was. Here, and ever since, he placed bolts only as a last resort.

The original premise of climbing—that all routes should be climbed from the ground up, without previewing—is, to Beyer, both ethic and religion. His traditional convictions are bred of twenty-three seasons in Yosemite, ten in the Tetons, and three in the Karakoram. He despairs of, and endorses, guerrilla warfare on the gridwork rap-bolting practices of sport climbers. Like the EarthFirst! environmentalists who creep into forests to hammer mill-saw-wrecking spikes into old-growth trees, he has, under cover of darkness, erased several efforts of the Bosch generation. "Anyone has the right to place a bolt wherever they want," he says, "but anyone is also free to remove it." In a letter to *Climbing* magazine, he challenged its editors to publish a "how-to" article on bolt removal to balance the plethora of advice on bolting, hangdogging, and sport-climbing techniques filling today's magazines. But the story of Jim Beyer, student of traditional ethics, pales against the tale of Jim Beyer, graduate of the school of hard knocks.

The year Beyer soloed *The Shield* he left Yosemite in a VW bug crammed with his possessions to climb in the Canadian Rockies. In Banff, while hanging around a parking lot outside a pub with a friend, Beyer was accosted by a man wearing a leather jacket. "He grabbed me by my sweater and cranked me up close to smell my breath," says Beyer. "Then he flashed a police badge." Ordered to empty his pockets, Beyer produced an apple. The undercover agent was disappointed; he was looking for contraband. But Beyer had a joint in his back pocket. His survival instinct took over. He backed out of his sweater, leaving it in the agent's hands and ran. Cutting his losses, the narc arrested Beyer's friend. After a cold bivouac in the woods, Beyer traded himself to the police for his buddy's release and spent a week in jail.

This youthful debacle ended when Beyer was deported, in handcuffs, from Canada as persona non grata. Once across the border he sped back to California, visited his girlfriend, found their relationship had ended, and proceeded to the haven of Yosemite. Near Merced, at 2 A.M., he parked the Bug and entered an orchard to sleep. When he awoke his car was gone; while he'd slept it had been burglarized, torched, then towed to the scrapyard. Beyer had lost everything he owned.

He quit climbing for a couple of years after that. "Jim's epic on *The Shield* really scared him, and a run of bad luck hit him hard," says Steve Quinlan, a climber and carpenter from Wyoming, and one of Beyer's oldest friends. "I think it shocked him to discover his capacity for getting himself into hot water."

So Beyer filled his life with other things. For a time he drifted with radical environmentalists. Later he earned a place on the U.S. National Kayak Team as a flatwater racer. Curious to examine left-wing politics from the inside, he visited Nicaragua with an American group after the Sandinista revolution, to help harvest the coffee crop. Beyer did not adapt well to his new surroundings, however, and he tired of the endless political lectures, barracks living, and constant surveillance. Instead of kowtowing to the propagandists, he argued with them. One day he rented a car and went to the beach, without official permission. Such independent thinking didn't rest well with his Sandinista hosts: he was deported from Nicaragua by armed escort.

Beyer's own tales created, for me, the picture of a loner. But people who know Beyer better reveal another side of the man.

"He is the most politically aware climber I've ever met," says Quinlan, who told me of Beyer's support over many years of environmental and political causes. On one occasion Beyer marched with a group from Moab to Salt Lake City, as a protest against a planned nuclear dump in the desert near North Six Shooter Peak. As for Beyer the climber, Quinlan affectionately describes a curmudgeonly reactionary traditionalist who refused to use spring-loaded camming devices for several years after they were invented, and who often didn't report his new routes, especially those in the Wind River Range.

By 1982 Beyer had quit believing he could find a more significant purpose in life than climbing. If he had abandoned climbing because he suspected its tunnel-visioned lifestyle made him unsuited to normal society, then he returned to it because it was the most gratifying life he knew. And when he returned to Yosemite it was to activate the plan he had been nurturing since his earliest solo walls. He embarked on a series of climbs that would harden him for his ultimate dream: a new route, solo, alpine style, boltless, in the Karakoram Range.

Methodically he ticked off a succession of new Yosemite walls. On *Heading for Oblivion* (VI A4+) on Leaning Tower he copperheaded his way up tenuous seams just 40 feet right of the original Harding route. But, unlike Harding, Beyer did little drilling. He regards this as his hardest Yosemite wall. Later, on a 23.5-hour roped solo of El Cap's west face, he accomplished the monolith's first one-day solo.

Solid Yosemite granite polished Beyer's technical skills, but to harden himself against isolation and pure terror he turned to the lofty and crumbling Fisher Towers near Moab, Utah. These lonely, weirdly eroded sandstone spires, says Beyer, are "an alien, hostile environment, perfect for training for the Karakoram." During the 1980s he forced himself up five new solo routes there, some up to 900 feet high.

To describe these routes he coined a term: "shakefest," a climb that reduces the leader to a state of quivering terror. Beyer's route names reflect his mindset at a given time: *Sandinista Couloir* and *Revolutionary Crest* from the Tetons in the early 1980s show his Nicaraguan period. In the Fisher Towers, his route names reflect a darker mood—*Run Amok* (VI, 5.9 A4a), *World's End* (VI 5.9 A5a), *Death of American Democracy* (VI 5.10 A4d), and *Deadmans' Party* (VI 5.10 A5c). On these, he conditioned himself to climb alone, and to never give up, no matter how scary or awful the climbing was. On *Run Amok*, in 1979, he climbed a pitch-length curtain of vertical dirt by chopping steps into it with a hammer. He looked at *Death of American Democracy* for five years before finding the gumption to try it. On it he discovered the use of aluminum heads in soft rock. Such placements, aid-climbing aficionados will attest, provide all the security of walking on thin ice in a heat wave. On *Intifada*, his masterpiece on the east face of Cottontail Tower, Beyer quivered enough to rate the route A6— it is perhaps the world's most severe aid route. He summarizes the delights of the last pitch as "thirty-eight hook moves, a crux of stacked blade tips in rotten flakes, and a lunge to the summit." Beyer used no bolts on the route, not even for belays.

Beyer's Conradian obsession with Fisher Towers scared not only him but also those close to him. "During those years," he says, "every girlfriend I had told me I'd die there."

The Fisher Towers attuned Beyer so well to the subtleties of aid placements that he subdivided aid ratings from the usual 5 into 14. In this system A1 through A3+ describe aid in a way most climbers who have stood in etriers would comprehend. Beyer's system divides A4 and above, though, into four degrees, a to d. Hard, or "psycho" aid commences at A4d, a rating that indicates the risk of a 40-foot fall with injury potential.

A5a sports 60-foot fall potential. By A5d a fall could rip out a full pitch, including the anchor. Beyer describes A6a as having "extreme death potential involving more than two pitches with possible 200-foot falls. Cruxes are cutting-edge technical aid. No bolts can be used for protection or belays, meaning that if you have fixed ropes below, a fall could rip out lower anchors, too."

Though Beyer generally climbed alone on his new routes, and quietly, word about these climbs got around the desert. Were his routes as extreme as he claimed? One veteran desert rat, Kyle Copeland, a climbing guide and guidebook author from Moab, knows Beyer and the nature of his routes. "There is no doubt that Jim has done the hardest nailing routes on Utah sandstone," he says, "but I don't always agree with his choice of line. He looks for incipience and difficulty rather than aesthetics."

Charlie Fowler, the peripatetic all-round climber from Telluride, Colorado, has known Beyer since the 1970s. "Jim has become a role model to many Yosemite big-wall climbers," he says. "He pushes hard on his routes. The few who know him find his single-mindedness inspiring."

But if Beyer's determination has earned him admiration, his intensity also scares people. "I'd be nervous to climb with Jim," says Copeland. "He might push me beyond my limits." Furthermore, though Beyer's routes are established from the ground up, he sometimes stretches the definition of traditional.

"Jim's tactics are unusual," says John Middendorf, a big-waller with many hard desert and Yosemite walls to his credit. "He sometimes fixes ropes until the final ascent, bivying on the ground rather than the wall. And his free tactics are questionable. He sometimes aids a pitch first then subsequently frees the moves while hanging on jumars from fixed rope."

Beyer admits to these methods in accounts in the *American Alpine Journal*. Of *Intifada* in the Fisher Towers he states "the 900-foot climb took nine days and one night on the wall." On a new route on El Capitan left of the west face, *Reach for the Sky* (VI 5.11d A4d), he records his tactic of working a pitch free from fixed rope. "My only question about climbing like that," Middendorf says, "is that subsequent leaders are unlikely to find themselves on-sighting 5.12 when the only pro is A3 copperheads that the first ascent party placed on aid, but subsequently removed."

After his sagas on the Fisher Towers, Beyer noticed something an impartial observer might call strange: he was more comfortable climbing alone than with a partner. "On multiday aid routes," he explained during our Boulder meeting, "you need mental stamina to focus on the technical situation. Being with another person breaks my concentration."

With the dream of a Karakoram wall of rock and ice in his mind, Beyer spent hundreds of hours running, weightlifting and biking. He crafted his diet to create physical bulk to sustain his body on long walls. Even on a simple pitch in Eldorado, he always shouldered a full rack to stay used to carrying the heavy gear needed on long routes.

In the mid-1980s he began experimenting with a form of sports meditation or self-hypnosis. "It's mental preprogramming," says Beyer. "It helps me cope with instants when I need an automatic reaction to survive." He would visualize himself in dangerous climbing situations and store survival responses. Long before a climb Beyer would be psychologically ready, for he had already visualized the worst a climb could present—even hideous injury. By indoctrinating himself with planned, automatic escapes from every situation he learned to push himself harder. "Some people buy insurance," he says. "I train mentally and physically to stay alive."

By 1989 Beyer deemed himself ready for the Karakoram. He arrived at the base of the Grand Cathedral, a 19,245-foot-high granite layer cake of walls overlooking the Baltoro Glacier. With only a cook at Base Camp as support, Beyer set off on his dream climb. At just about the same time Mark Wilford and I stumbled out from a 13-day nightmare of storm and failure on Nameless Tower. Once again, as in Yosemite in 1977, I found myself on the ground, watching Beyer, who appeared as a dot on the wall. Beyer's cook, a Balti, handed me a cup of tea and we sat on a boulder watching him solo a searing crack line. "Jim good man," said the cook, "but little bit crazy."

Fifty-four pitches. Thirteen days. Beyer's route on Grand Cathedral was no pushover but it went smoothly in good weather. He rated the experience VII 5.10d A4+. Perhaps it was a fantasy realized too easily, for in 1990 he was back in the Karakoram, this time in the Hunza region.

"On some of my climbs I've gone for the summit at all costs, exceeding what could be called intelligent actions. This might compromise my credibility with some people," said Beyer as he began to tell me the story of his solo of *Bib-O-li-Motin*, a 19,685-foot rock fang above the village of Karimabad.

I, too, knew the peak well. I'd attempted it in 1985, but fusillades of stonefall from its couloirs and 2,200-foot walls sent me and my companions running, as it did three later expeditions. The only previous ascent of the mountain when Beyer tried it in 1990 was by Patrick Cordier's French party in 1982, via the mixed East Ridge. The stupendous southeast face was unclimbed, and that was Beyer and Pat McInerny's goal.

Beyer had befriended McInerny, a climbing guide, that year in Moab. To prepare for the Karakoram the two climbed a new route on The Diamond (*Steep is Flat*, VI 5.10 A4+), and had an impressive season in the French Alps. On *Bib-O-li-Motin*, the pair spent 12 dangerous days dodging rockfall, fixing rope, and load-carrying up a 200-foot ice cliff in the approach couloir before dumping their gear at the foot of the wall. Large avalanches are common in this region—two Japanese attempts on Ultar, a peak next to *Bib- O-li-Motin* have ended tragically this way, and in 1985 I'd seen slides rake the gullies and flow over the meadows sweeping away sheep and goats.

The night Beyer and McInerny set off they found their fixed ropes piled at the foot of the ice cliff, shredded by an avalanche. Undeterred, Beyer patched a makeshift line together from bits of 5- and 9-millimeter cord and headed back up the ice cliff at the final overhanging lip. Beyer, totally without protection because all their gear was beneath the wall, found rotten ice that he couldn't get his ice tools to stick in. Each time he struck his ice tools or kicked a crampon into it, the ice exploded and his placement skated. A shakefest began that Beyer calls "worse than A6." Says McInerny, "It was the most incredible thing I've ever seen. For five minutes Jim would dangle from one ice axe, get the other in, then the first would pop out, along with his feet. He was gasping desperately. If he'd fallen he'd have gone 200 feet, and the rope would surely have snapped."

But eventually Beyer fought his way over the bulge. The pair reached the wall in a storm and began to climb. Two days later it was still storming and they were 500 feet up, climbing rotten rock. Cold numbed their hands. McInerny dropped a rope. As he rigged a rappel to fetch it from a rock snag, his doubts about the sanity of their adventure welled to the surface.

"Maybe I'll just rap down to the rope and keep going and let you solo this nightmare," McInerny said. "Why don't you do that," replied Beyer calmly.

The partnership they'd begun on The Diamond was hard for McInerny to break. "I felt bad leaving Jim," McInerny later told me, "I wanted to be there, but I was way out of my depth."

As McInerny began the first rappel Beyer smiled at him reassuringly, to let him know he bore no grudge. "Don't worry, dude," he said in a fatherly tone. "You're like 99 percent of the people. You're afraid of dying."

By day six Beyer was near the top, having climbed a dozen ice-coated free and aid pitches. But three days later he hadn't moved, trapped in his bivy sack as a snowstorm raged around him. On the ninth day he pressed on in frigid weather. Beyer's resolve and equipment were now wearing thin. His ropes were frozen cables, his ice hammer had snapped at the head, his food was dwindling, and the weather, by the tenth evening, was again deteriorating. The whole time Beyer was on the wall a Japanese expedition on Ultar deemed the weather so bad they didn't move out of Base Camp.

"Every hour or two," says Beyer, "I'd stop and shout into the storm, 'Do I really want to go on?'" Each time he decided he did, he'd swallow a caffeine pill and continue.

Sixty feet from the top he found himself stemming free up a rime-coated dihedral, his boots skating. Suddenly the snow blobs forming his footholds collapsed and he was hurtling through the air.

Self-belayed falls tend to be long and often messy, and Beyer could ill-afford such folly. His mental programming kicked into gear. He rotated and lunged for his last piece of pro and caught it with both hands. Had this catch been in a baseball game, Beyer would have received the MVP award, but where he was his only reward was survival. Grappling with the corner again, he thrashed up and over the rim to find himself in darkness and storm, without headlamp or bivouac gear. He was not, however, on top but on a rubble-strewn slope below a thorny crown of possible summits.

The situation was deflating. "My adrenaline rush had long gone," says Beyer. "The survivor in me said, 'No more.'" He turned around.

Bitter thoughts wracked Beyer on the descent. He felt he no longer cared about summits. He hated mountains. But by the time he reached the meadows and McInerny two days later, he realized that, although he hadn't stood on the highest pile of rubble on top, his climb by all other measures was a success: he had completed a wall that had thwarted four expeditions, and he and his partner were going home alive.

By 1991 Beyer figured he was ready to climb the hardest big-wall route in the world. Using money from a spec-house he built in Boulder, he organized an expedition to Nameless Tower (20,463 feet) in Pakistan, and, since he was in the land of the 8,000-meter peaks, Gasherbrum I (aka Hidden Peak, 26,471 feet). Two solo "training" routes, in 1989 and 1990 in Colorado's Black Canyon of the Gunnison—*Climb Bold or Fly* on the Painted Wall, and *Black Planet* on North Chasm View Wall, both boltless and rated VI A4d—had put him in good stead.

Perhaps *Bib-O-li-Motin* had left a residue of fear in him. Shortly before departing for Pakistan, Beyer visited Yosemite to seek a partner for Nameless Tower. John Middendorf was keen. Though Middendorf had seen Beyer around for years and knew he was a master big-wall climber they'd only climbed a few short free routes together. "Jim was always an outsider to the cliques of Yosemite," says Middendorf, who suggested they climb a long route to get better acquainted. Beyer and Middendorf's Pakistan plan, however, never got off the ground.

Beyer arrived alone in Islamabad a few weeks after the defeat of Saddam Hussein's army. Many climbers had canceled their trips to Islamic Pakistan. Not Beyer. He called his expedition the Trango Shakefest '91. He wanted an experience beyond any of his other climbs. This he got, but not in the way he planned.

His problems began in Islamabad. Says Beyer, "A paperwork mix-up between my expedition and some other group had led my young liaison officer (LO) to believe three women were on my team. His first question to me was, 'Where are the ladies?' When I explained there was only me, his fantasy of a vacation in a Base Camp of women was shattered."

To fathom Beyer's further fiascos one must understand that Pakistan's mountaineering rules in 1991 required expeditions to have at least four members. Through negotiations with the Ministry of Tourism, Beyer solved this glitch by hiring three Pakistani high-altitude porters to be his partners. It wasn't an ideal situation, and was costly, but it got Beyer moving toward the mountains. The problem was, though paid and contracted to do so, this trio refused to carry loads. During the approach along the Baltoro, these paid members and Beyer's other porters made daily sit-down strikes, demanding better equipment and more pay.

But Beyer's main conflicts arose from the bad chemistry between him and his LO, whom Beyer paints as a rigid martinet who protested at every opportunity.

"Jim, you'll take 101 risks on this climb, but I will not take a single risk," said the LO at the start of the trip. "Every rule must be followed exactly." Things went downhill from there, says Beyer, beginning when the LO, while examining the expedition clothing provided by Beyer, found he was getting used longjohns and other hand-me-downs from Beyer's wardrobe. The combination of the LO's intractability and Beyer's distrust of authority figures and naivete on how to interact with his Pakistani hosts created an explosive situation. (The LO was unavailable for comment for this article.)

Perhaps Beyer had preprogrammed himself for the showdown that followed on the Dunge Glacier. On the final day of the approach, trouble began within sight of the granite bulwark of Nameless Tower. Beyer attempted to pay off and send back one of his three paid members. This plan—intended to save him money and endorsed by the Ministry of Tourism, says Beyer—precipitated an argument when the member refused to leave. He wanted to stay to earn more money. Backed up by the LO, the others quit in sympathy, leaving Beyer with six regular porters to shuttle his 10 loads to the peak. Beyer left the four bickering on the talus fields, and set off, happy to be rid of them. An hour later, sweating under a heavy load, Beyer heard the LO behind him hailing the group to stop.

Awaiting the LO's arrival, Beyer instructed the porters to remove their loads and pile them in a heap. "No man approaches me," he ordered, and positioned them ten feet away.

"The expedition is over," declared the LO. "We return to Skardu. Porters, pick up your loads and follow me."

"Don't touch the loads. Everyone stand back," Beyer countered.

The LO had found a technical point; because three members had quit, Beyer was no longer the team of four stipulated by the rules. Also illegal was the fact that the team had split into two groups. Such details are commonly overlooked by LOs, who usually seek to help an expedition climb its peak. But in this case expedition justice became perverted.

A war of words ensued. Beyer made it clear he was staying. Essentially, he was in the right—the rules state that the expedition leader is the ultimate authority, and if he disagrees with an LO's decision he must state the nature of the disagreement in writing, but need not follow the LO's orders.

Meanwhile a witness appeared out of the rubble: a Spanish climber heading up to jumar his ropes on Great Trango Tower. "He seemed torn between his climb and this crazy spectacle," says Beyer. "I said, 'Hey, man, wait a few minutes and you'll see the biggest fistfight of all time.' I knew I couldn't fight off ten guys, but a witness might be useful."

The Spaniard left. With a cry of, "Porters, follow me," the LO charged at Beyer, who threw the enraged soldier onto his back. Successive charges—unaided by the flabbergasted Balti porters—ended identically.

"You assaulted a Pakistan army lieutenant," the LO screamed. "I vow you will never leave this country. You will go to jail. I will see that a helicopter returns to forcibly remove you from this mountain."

Beyer considered, then stared into the LO's eyes and said calmly, "The decisions you make today might have a great effect on your career, Lieutenant, because if a helicopter comes up here they'll never take me alive."

While relating the tale to me Beyer grinned, as if in hindsight he had found a soft spot for the LO. "We were similar in a way. We're both fearless." The stalemate ended when Beyer agreed that everyone but he would return to Skardu. He gave the Pakistanis food and a goat, but retained everything else.

Alone, Beyer couldn't shake off the feeling that his enemies were hiding in the rocks, waiting to steal his gear the moment he left camp. So he hid his loads under boulders across the glacier, and carried them up-valley by night to a concealed camp where he hid by day from the threatened helicopter (which never materialized). After a week of load-carrying to the base of the 3000-foot wall Beyer was in position to begin the greatest climb of his life. He had gone through the awful and the absurd to get there; now it was just himself and the wall. In a fit of jubilation he stood atop a boulder and declared the Dunge Glacier an independent country, and himself its benevolent dictator.

But as Beyer climbed the couloir next evening he was flooded by doubts. "With every step toward the wall a voice inside me kept saying, 'Dude, you are one step closer to death,' says Beyer. The insanity of the previous weeks and the isolation were playing on his nerves, but Beyer knew the value of intuition. To add to his burdens he had twisted his ankle (the injury was later diagnosed as a fracture), and walked with pain throughout the week of load-carrying.

Beyer gropes for words to explain his snap decision to quit Nameless Tower. "I spent a lot of time in my tent, thinking. Climbing had always been something I'd done for my own amusement," he says. "But this time I'd found myself fighting for the very right to do it. Every step of the way things had gone wrong, and I began to have very negative thoughts about my chances under the emotional circumstances. One morning I woke up with a complete change of thought. I would cross the glacier, find some people to talk to, and head on to a fresh start and another adventure: to climb an 8,000-meter peak."

Masquerading as a trekker hurrying to catch his friends, Beyer and a single porter he hired on the Baltoro Glacier trail crept through Base Camps to arrive beneath Broad Peak (26,400 feet), the world's twelfth highest summit. He had abandoned the idea of Gasherbrum I, for which he had a permit, as it was two additional days up-valley. Beyer planned a clandestine ascent, using fixed ropes and camps others had left on Broad Peak's west face. He began climbing the day after his arrival, just as storm clouds appeared. It was late in the season and his camp had minimal provisions. Beyer gambled that he could climb faster than the storm would advance.

Carrying only a bivy sack, he raced up the slopes. At about 23,000 feet he encountered three Frenchmen descending from the impending storm.

"Who are you?" one asked, shocked to see a new face on the hill.

"I can't tell you my name, but I am your friend," said Beyer, still edgy about being captured by the army.

"American?" quizzed the Frenchman.

"I am your friend."

"You have no permit?"

"I'm a friend. Tell me what is above."

"There are some Mexicans, but their tents are full."

"I have no tent, no sleeping bag," explained Beyer.

"You must go down!" shouted the Frenchman.

"Not till I reach the summit."

"You are crazy!" The French climbers left.

At the Mexican tent a gale howled. Beyer, desperately cold, shouted into the door, "Buenos días. I'm in bad shape out here." He had weighed the possibilities of this moment. What if the Mexicans refused him entry? Would he beg them, bribe them, use violence? He didn't have to worry. Two hands reached out and dragged him in. For an hour Beyer languished in exhaustion—he hadn't eaten or drunk all day, and had climbed 8,000 feet.

But soon the tent began disintegrating in the hurricane wind, and the Mexicans urged him to get out and escape with them. When he looked out at the raging storm, Beyer realized climbing up was impossible and began descending. His first few steps told him that his body had, as endurance athletes put it, "bonked," or used up every molecule of available energy. Hallucinations and leg cramps plagued him. He staggered, sobbing with the pain and frustration and fear that his body wouldn't carry him out of the blizzard. Beyer became convinced he'd die. The Mexicans urged him on, but the snows were nearly smothering them and they didn't even know who he was. The only thing that kept him awake during that ten-hour descent to Camp 2 were his caffeine pills, each one equivalent to two cups of coffee.

"I'd always prided myself on being a survivor, and it was those skills, that willpower and all my training that got me down that afternoon," says Beyer. "But I also realized something else, and that was how much I love life. Anyone who didn't want to live as much as me would have died, regardless of their training."

At Camp 2 Beyer flopped in a tent while the Mexicans descended to Base Camp. Twenty hours of constant movement had wrecked him. He stayed awake long enough to melt some snow and drink it. At dawn he awoke to a churning gut. The snow—polluted by many climbers over many seasons—had given him explosive diarrhea. "The stomach cramps were terrible. I fouled the tent, my suit, everything." He forced himself down the last of the mountain, shit welling up the legs of his altitude suit. At basecamp he collapsed, until the Mexican team's doctor rendered assistance.

Oh, were it over then; he had yet to face the music in Islamabad after walking out. Needless to say, the Ministry of Tourism's officials didn't view Shakefest '91 as a triumph in U.S.–Pakistan relations. Wisely, they'd vetoed the LO's demand for a helicopter mission to arrest Beyer, but when Beyer asked them to refund his helicopter-rescue and environmental-protection bonds (amounts totaling $5,000) matters got sticky.

At the Ministry, a high-ranking official told Beyer "The good news is we won't stop you leaving the country. The bad news is your LO says your porter did massive environmental damage on their hike out by burning firewood and not disposing of a goat carcass in a hygienic manner."

Pressed to sign a document accepting responsibility and forfeiting $1,000, Beyer refused, calling the charge bogus. An argument ensued, which became so heated that Beyer's Pakistani trekking agent, who was also present, shouted, "I hate Americans! George Bush kills innocent Iraqis!"

Finally Beyer consented to pay a small fine. "Well, Mr. Beyer," said the Ministry of Tourism official as the troublesome tourist left his office, "I don't think we'll be seeing you back in Pakistan again, will we?"

My weekend with Beyer was classic Colorado, with cool winter sunshine. He took most of a day to relate his tale of Pakistan, and by its end he looked exhausted. In what he'd told me I found much that was shocking and askew from my perceptions of human nature. Though I admire Beyer in the same way I admire climbers like Voytek Kurtyka, Doug Scott, and Mugs Stump, his cult of solitude was unsettling in a visceral way. But then I had never visited the spiritual and physical hinterlands of self the way he had. Beyer had many layers, and I had only scratched the surface of getting to know him. Though his adventures as a soloist defined a personality separate from those around him, at my last question he revealed a newly emergent individual.

"I'll ask you the question I'm often asked after an expedition," I had said to Beyer. "Are you a different person than before that ordeal?"

It sounded like a dumb question, and I expected to hear plans of more solo brinkmanship. Instead he said this: "I left the old Jim behind the morning I decided to quit Nameless Tower. It's not that I psyched out, but for the first time I admitted to myself I was wrong. My whole psychology believed it was right to cultivate risks to achieve success. This led me to take terrible chances. Because I was soloing, in my self-centered world I could talk myself into it. Without being conscious of it, I behaved as if summits were worth dying for. I don't buy that anymore."

I hadn't counted on this dimension of Beyer—sobered, humble, sated. When he saw I was surprised he simplified his reasoning: "I guess I just saw clearly that someday a hook was going to pop when I was soloing and that would be the end. I still want to climb hard and climb traditionally but I want to share it—with partners."

Jim Beyer, soloing again in the late 1990s, comes prepared to do battle with the rock— and win. PHOTO: BEYER COLLECTION

THE FIRST SOLO ASCENT OF MOUNT EVEREST

by Reinhold Messner

When Mount Everest was first climbed in 1953, an army of Sherpas and mountaineers assailed the peak with miles of rope, tons of food, ladders, bottled oxygen, radios, and everything earthly possible to secure the top. Twenty-seven years later, Reinhold Messner, with only the pack on his back and the scant breath in his lungs, soloed to the top of the world's highest mountain. He carried no extras, not even a radio to communicate with his Base Camp crew, which consisted only of his girlfriend. The first person to ascend all fourteen of the world's 8,000-meter peaks, Messner revolutionized Himalayan mountaineering, supplanting large-scale siege tactics with lightweight, self-contained squads (sometimes consisting of only himself and one other partner) and rapid-fire ascents. Having long foregone the support previous generations had considered fundamental, this time Messner dispensed with the most basic component in a mountaineer's arsenal: a partner. In this ultimate triumph of self-reliance, Reinhold Messner crowned a climbing career which may never be equaled.

‡   ‡   ‡

Suddenly the snow gave under me. My headlamp went out. I fell into the abyss—in slow motion, or so I experienced it—striking the ice walls once with my back, once with my chest. My sense of time was gone. Had I been falling seconds or was it already minutes? Suddenly there was ground under my feet again. Now I knew I was trapped in a crevasse on the side of Mount Everest—perhaps forever!

I should have taken a radio with me. Then I would have been able to call Nena, whom I had left far below at five o'clock that morning, at our advanced base camp at 6,500 meters. Nena Holguin was an experienced mountaineer and could have climbed up here and let a rope down to free me from this icy prison. But a radio weighed as much as three gas cartridges, and fuel for my cooker seemed more important than the possibility of being able to call for help.

I thumbed on my headlamp, put my head back and saw, about eight meters above me, a tree-trunk-sized hole through which glimmered a few stars. The iridescent blue-green ice walls, some two meters apart, soared up toward each other. Then I knew I could not get out. I flashed my torch into the depths of the crevasse but there was no end to it. The snow bridge that had broken my fall was only a square-meter wide. Lucky, I thought; but now my whole body was trembling with terror. I wondered if I could don my crampons on the shaky snow support, but with each movement fear of plunging deeper overwhelmed me. Then I discovered a ramp that led obliquely upward toward the porthole of stars. Climbing the ramp, I made my way once again to the upper surface of the glacier in a few minutes—but I was still on the valley side of the gaping crevasse, downhill from the storied face I had set out to climb. And I was alone.

Trance-like, I went back to the hole through which I had disappeared ten minutes before. Dawn light illuminated the North Col of Mount Everest. I looked at my watch: it was shortly before seven. The fall into the crevasse had snapped me wide awake. I knew there was only this one spot where I could cross the crevasse, which cut right across the 300-meter-high ice wall under the North Col. Four weeks before, in July on my first reconnaissance march to the 7,000-meter-high North Col, I had discovered this snow bridge, just two meters wide. At that time it had borne my weight. It had to hold up briefly now because, on my solo ascent, I had no aluminum ladders and ropes with me to facilitate the crossing. Two ski sticks and my light alloy ice axe were my only aids. On the other side the crevasse was a steep snow wall. I bent forward and inserted the ski sticks, handles foremost, high on the wall. Then I swung myself across. I knew that more than ten mountaineers had lost their lives on the slopes of the North Col.

Daylight grew. Far in the east, above a blue-gray sea of mist, stood the mighty massif of Kanchenjunga. It had been wise to break off my attempt in July. The snow, softened by the warm monsoon, had seemed bottomless and the avalanche danger great. Now, on August 18, the snow was firmly frozen and good to walk on.

The pale dawn lay over the summit of Mount Everest, towering so clear against the deep blue sky that I could easily recognize the freestanding rock tower on the North-East Ridge. There George Mallory and Andrew Irvine were last seen on their bold summit push in 1924. Nobody knew whether the pair had perished during the ascent or the descent. Had they indeed reached the summit? Were they the first to climb the highest mountain in the world, which the Tibetans call Chomolungma, "Goddess Mother of the World"?

The British had been the first to attempt climbing Mount Everest. After a large-scale reconnaissance in 1921 the original assault was made a year later up the route I was now climbing. With poor equipment by today's standards—gear with which I would not climb the tourist route on the Matterhorn!—Mallory and his friends Norton and Somervell passed the 8,000-meter barrier for the first time in the history of mountaineering. That fiery spirit George Mallory realized then that Mount Everest had to be stormed in six days from the Rongbuk Monastery Base Camp (5,100 meters), after thorough preparation and six weeks of acclimatization. Two years later Mallory was dead. But the attempts on the Tibetan north side of Mount Everest went on until the Second World War, after which the Chinese closed the frontier to foreigners, achieving the first ascent via the North Col themselves in 1960, and again in 1975.

In the spring of 1980 they opened the frontier. The Japanese, with a major expedition, were the first after the Chinese to make the summit up the northern route. Shortly after them I had reached Base Camp via Lhasa and Shigatse. Seven weeks had passed. On the journey to Base Camp I had accumulated many impressions of Tibet, a country of pastel colors and endless distances. This was the land of my dreams. At the same time it had often depressed me. From the whitewashed mud houses with the black window apertures, Tibetan prayer flags no longer waved, only red rags. The monastery at Rongbuk, earlier inhabited by 400 monks, was now empty. Plundered. Thousands of paintings had been peeled from the decaying walls. The roofs of the temple were staved in. In the mountain villages I'd seen poor, apathetic faces. Here the people did not laugh as in the mountains of Nepal.

The altimeter showed 7,360 meters. It was about nine o'clock. Now I was climbing more slowly. The stretch to the North Col I had done in two hours and so was able to spare myself one bivouac. Now and then the snow was ankle deep, and the snowdrifts cost energy. I could not afford to exhaust myself or I'd pay for the effort tomorrow and the day after.

My ski sticks were a big help; with their aid I could distribute my weight on arms and legs.

The northern slope to my right was a huge expanse of snow with dark islands of rock. Clearly recognizable were avalanche tracks. For the time being I stayed on the blunt North Ridge. That was the safest route. No trace of my predecessors. Everything was buried under a thick mantle of snow. Only once, at about 7,500 meters, did I see a red rope in the snow anchored to a rock island. On these ropes the Japanese team had descended to Base Camp when the weather turned bad; up them they had been able to climb hand over hand to continue the ascent.

By these tactics I had already climbed Mount Everest in 1978, via the southern route. This time I had nobody to assist me with carrying or to prepare my bivouac, no companions to help break trail in the deep snow. Every last task was for me to accomplish alone.

Like a snail with its house on its back, I carried my tent in my rucksack. I would pitch it, sleep in it and take it with me for the next night. A second tent would have been too heavy. My fifteen kilos felt so heavy at this altitude that I stopped after a dozen paces, gasped for breath and forgot everything around me. The stretches between rest pauses became shorter. Each time it required great willpower to stand up again after a breather. Step by step I tormented myself as far as 7,800 meters. I had the feeling of someone behind encouraging me.

The first campsite which I stamped out in the snow did not please me. I had to camp on rock to be able to adequately anchor the tent. A few meters below I saw an ideal spot but I lacked the strength to unpack my rucksack and repitch the tent. I sat there and gazed down to advanced Base Camp whence I had set off at five o'clock that morning. It was now after three in the afternoon. I recognized a tiny red patch. Nena must have placed the sleeping bag on the roof of the tent to protect herself from the heat. Up to now the heat had been worse than the cold. At night the thermometer dropped only to -10 degrees C in Base Camp; up here to -20 degrees C. During the day the sun dehydrated me. The oxygen-thin air rasped my throat. I remembered that I had a tiny bottle of Japanese herb with me and put a couple of drops on my tongue. That gave relief for a while and opened the air passages. Apart from aspirin, this herbal remedy was the only medication I took.

Nena must be able to see me with her binoculars. I hoped she wasn't worried. Before the start I had explained to her that there should be no problems if on the first day I made more than 1,200 meters height. On my solo ascent of Nanga Parbat two years before, which had given me the psychological foundation for this solo trip to Everest, I was only able to climb 1,600 meters the first day, but then I had started from 4,800 meters. There was a vast difference between climbing at 6,000 and 7,000 meters above sea level. Here each and every small maneuver was an effort.

My tiny tent, not two kilos in weight and constructed so that it could withstand storms up to 100 kilometers per hour, did not require much space. If I bent my legs, it was just big enough to lie in. I had trouble pitching it because time and again a gust of wind blew in and lifted it up. I anchored it with ski sticks, an ice axe and the only rock piton I had with me. I laid a finger-thick foam mat on the floor. For a while I simply lay there and listened to the wind hurling ice crystals against the tent wall. It was coming from the northwest. That was a good sign: the weather should hold.

I knew I ought to cook. But I was so tired by the many small preparations for the night that I could not rouse myself to do it, although I had eaten nothing since morning. I thought of Maurice Wilson, a religious fanatic, who in 1934 had attempted a solo ascent of Everest. Although he had been no climber, he remained steadfastly convinced that God would lead him up Everest and had not given up after the terrible snowstorms and several falls. On his first run up to the North Col he had not been able to cover the stretch from advanced Base Camp to the col at 7,000 meters in four days, as he had planned. At the end of his strength, he had crawled back to his last camp where two porters awaited him. They had known he would not make it and tried to persuade him to give up. But when he was on his legs again, the madman had climbed up once more. A year later his corpse was found at the foot of the North Col. The last lines of his diary read: "Off again, gorgeous day."

Was I just as mad as Wilson, obsessed by an idea which nobody understood, not even mountaineers? I had already climbed Mount Everest once. Why endure the risk and drudgery a second time? Yet I knew that, because I was alone this time, it was a different mountain altogether—even though it had the same summit.

"Fai la cucina," someone near me was saying, "Get into the kitchen." I thought again about cooking. I talked half aloud to myself. The strong feeling of being with an invisible companion led me to hope that the other person was doing the cooking. I asked myself how we would have space enough to sleep in this tiny tent. I wanted to divide the first piece of dried meat which I fetched out of my rucksack into two equal portions. I spoke in Italian, although for me, as a South Tyroler, my mother tongue was German. For three months I had been speaking only English with my Canadian friend Nena. Such was my confusion.

The wind had become so strong that the tent fluttered and every time I opened the entrance a hands-breadth—to shovel snow with the lid of my cooking pot—it blew out the flame on my gas cooker. It will be a bad night, I thought.

It takes a lot of snow to melt a liter of water. At first I made tomato soup, then two pots of Tibetan salt tea which I had learned to prepare from the nomads. A palmfull of herbs to a liter of water and two pinches of salt. I had to drink a lot: four liters a day if I were not to dry out.

The cooking lasted some hours. I just lay there, held the cooking pot and pushed a piece of dried meat or Parmesan cheese in my mouth. With it I chewed hard South Tyrol Bauernbrot, a coarse brown bread. All these small actions added up to a bodily ordeal.

I lay with my clothes in my sleeping bag, dozing. When I opened my eyes I did not know whether it was morning or evening, but I did not want to look at my watch. Deep down I was anxious. It was not fear of anything in particular which seized me, it was all the experiences of my mountaineering life, the exertion of thirty years of climbing awake in me. Avalanches, states of exhaustion I had experienced—they all condensed now into an extensive, deep-seated anxiety. I knew what could befall me up here. I knew how great the drudgery would be under the summit. Had I not known it, how could I have brought myself, hour after hour, step by step, to go on?

As the sun struck the tent in the morning and licked the hoarfrost from the inside, I packed everything again, leaving behind two tins of sardines and a gas cartridge as well as half the soup and tea. I must make do with the rest of the provisions. The weather was good. The next day I had to be on the summit.

For the first fifty meters I was slow; then I found my rhythm again and made good progress. I was climbing somewhat to the right of the North Ridge and the ground became steeper and steeper. I stuck fast in the snow and progressed slowly until I came to a place where an avalanche had broken away. To the right on the north face I saw my chance. The whole slope was one big avalanche track—there I would be able to move fast enough. I reassured myself that after two weeks of fine weather there was no danger of avalanche, that the snow had consolidated up above. And it seemed as though the weather would still hold for a couple of days. So I began a long, easily rising traverse, with many pauses.

What with the exertion and concentration, I had not noticed that the weather had turned bad. My surroundings were shrouded in mist. The peaks below had flattened out and I moved with the feeling of no longer belonging to the world beneath. When I looked at the altimeter at three o'clock in the afternoon, near the Norton Couloir, I despaired. It showed only 8,220 meters. I would gladly have gone on further but there was no bivouac site. Besides, I was too tired, so there I stayed.

An hour later, my tent stood on a rock outcrop. I had given up taking pictures. It took too much energy to screw the camera on the ice axe and set it, to walk away ten paces and wait for the click of the delayed action release. It was much more important that I make myself something to drink.

The snow had turned to ice at the edge of the rocks. I was sure it thawed in high summer when it was windless and misty, even on the summit of Everest. Nevertheless I must not be careless because at this height a few degrees of frost would cause frostbite. What should I do in the morning if the thickening mist had not dispersed? Should I wait and see? No, that was crazy. At this height one's body and mind only deteriorated, things could only get worse. The day after tomorrow I'd be so weakened that a summit assault would be impossible. I had to either go up or go down. There was no other choice.

Twice while melting snow I took my pulse. Way over 100 beats per minute. The night lasted a long time. I kept my clumsy double-layered boots on so that they did not cool down.

The morning of August 20th I left everything behind; even my rucksack stayed in the tent, but after a short while I missed it like a true friend. It had been my conversation partner, it had encouraged me to go on when I had been completely exhausted. Lack of oxygen and a blood-starved brain were the cause of these irrational experiences which I had got to know on my solo ascent of Nanga Parbat. Up here, in 1933, British climber Frank Smythe had shared his biscuits with an imaginary partner. The rucksack had been my companion but without it I got along much better. And my second friend, the ice axe, was still with me.

The way up the Norton Couloir was not too difficult. A snow gully led to a steep step shot through with brightly colored rock. In the middle there was a narrow ribbon of snow which made the ascent easier. An avalanche had swept down here not too long before, so the snow bore my weight. Soon it became softer and my speed decreased. On hands and knees I climbed upward like a tired dog, completely indifferent, the route never ending. By the time I was standing on a ledge below the summit, the mist was so thick that I could scarcely orient myself. A dark, vertical rock wall above barred the way but something drew me to the left and I made a small detour around the obstacle.

Over the next three hours I lost all track of time. Whenever a patch of blue sky appeared through the thick clouds I thought I saw the summit, and yet I was still amazed when suddenly the aluminum tripod—the summit indicator of Everest—stood before me, barely sticking out above the snow. The Chinese had anchored it here in 1975, in order to take exact measurements. I squatted down, feeling as heavy as lead. A scrap of frozen cloth was wrapped round the tripod. I must take some pictures, I told myself, as if repeating a formula. But I could not rouse myself to it for a long time.

I was not disappointed that, once again, enshrouded in clouds and mist, I had no real view from the summit of Mount Everest. For the second time I was on the highest point on earth and could see nothing. It was completely windless and the clouds welled around me, as if the earth was pulsating underneath. I did not know how I had done it but I knew that I could do no more. I could only stand up to go down.

FOOL'S GOAL: SHAWANGUNK SOLO CLIMBS

by Russ Clune

*S*olo ascents of titanic Asian mountains are dreams cast on the largest
possible earthly scale. Such climbs are often extended and involved. When
written up, a certain sameness of events can sometimes make the account
seem as diffuse as storm clouds streaming off an 8,000-meter summit. On the
other hand, ropeless ascents of short, world-class standard rock climbs strike like
bolts of lightning, with all the essence of life and death focused down to a small
and otherwise meaningless stretch of stone. The solo mountaineer might survive
a foot slipping or a fall into shallow crevasse. But if a climber soloing a difficult,
top-end rock climb so much as blinks at the wrong time, he is almost certainly
going to fall off and die. In the following account, Russ Clune, among the most
prolific and well-traveled climbers of the 1970s and 1980s, describes several high-
wire soloing acts at the Shawangunks in upstate New York, one of America's
most storied crags.

‡   ‡   ‡

At the belay below the crux roof of *Fat City*, a Gunks 5.10, Jeff Gruenberg
announced to his partners, "Someday I'm gonna solo this thing." But
when he followed it a few minutes later, he popped off the down-sloping
holds. Jeff dangled in the air and looked up at his friends. "Well, maybe
I'll make that a roped solo."

On a warm Friday evening about a year later, Jeff was again at the
crux roof of *Fat City*—only this time he didn't have his rope. It was an
impressive solo. Soon afterward, Dan McMillan climbed *Erect Direction*,

another 5.10, sans rope. The feat had been attempted before by another climber; his efforts had left him stranded light years off the deck, hanging by a single small nut in a corner below massive roofs. Dan had done the route a week earlier with a partner. "It felt so casual. I just wanted to solo it."

A new game had come to town. Although nothing was overt, a third-classing competition had started within a small clique of Gunks regulars.

Jeff and I agreed there were three ultraclassic solos: *Foops*, *Open Cockpit* and *Supercrack*. Whenever we were at Skytop, we found ourselves doing the three routes again and again. *Foops*, a famous 5.11 roof, felt solid. *Open Cockpit*, a slightly overhung, 40-foot 5.11+ face climb, was dicey. *Supercrack*, a 5.12 finger-wrencher, was out of the question: we still fell on it when we climbed it.

A sunny autumn afternoon brought me out to Skytop. I decided to give *Foops* a look. No one was around and I enjoyed the solitude. I climbed the 50-foot 5.9 wall to the base of the overhang and contemplated the chalk marks extending to the lip. After testing the first couple of holds, I returned to the rest and thought some more.

I heard boisterous conversation—a small group of tourists appeared in the talus below. Someone exclaimed, "Look!" I glanced down and saw a finger pointed at me. They grew silent and sat down among the boulders. I imagined I was in an auto race, the spectators waiting for me to crash and burst into flames. I waited them out. It felt an eternity. After they bored of watching paint dry, they left. I downclimbed; the mood was shattered.

Once again, it was a warm Friday evening when Jeff found himself alone on *Foops*. Once again, it was a momentous accomplishment: he'd ticked the first of the masterpiece solos.

That stirred up the scene. All the talk was becoming action. Naturally, we denied there was any competition involved. After all, what's the fascination in soloing something that's been unmercifully wired, a route where you know every move like the back of your hand? But while we said, "No big deal," we thought to ourselves, "Holy shit!" Nothing much was said about coming attractions, but the clique knew what was bound to happen sometime in the foreseeable future.

Jeff and I were on *Supercrack* (5.12). I redpointed it, set up a toprope and lowered down. Jeff waltzed through and belayed me from the top. I did another lap, removing the gear along the way. "This is really getting easy," I thought. Jeff had a smirk on his face when I pulled over the top. "So, when ya gonna solo it?" he asked expectantly. "Never. What's the point? What would it prove?" I said. "I have it so wired. Now, if somebody third-classed it on sight, that'd be impressive." Regardless of what I told Jeff, the idea of soloing *Supercrack* became a goal.

Jeff pulled another coup when he broke from the sacred three. *Open Cockpit* was the natural successor to *Foops*. Instead, he opted for *Yellow Wall*, a 5.11 that weaves through forbidding overhangs on less-than-the-best rock. A brilliant solo by any measure.

On a cloudy midweek day I meandered out to Skytop with just my shoes and chalkbag. I told myself I'd look for friends and climb whatever people were doing, but I knew the place would be deserted. It almost was. John Harlin and his wife, Adele, were climbing a route in the vicinity of *Open Cockpit*. "Hmm, *Open Cockpit*," I thought. I stood below it, then slipped my shoes on. Adele came around. I started up, chatting with her. Somehow her presence made me feel at ease. Whether it was because it kept my mind off what I was doing or it was just nice to have company, I'm not sure. I kept going: we kept talking.

When I was three-quarters up the face, Adele made a concerned inquiry. "Are you going to solo it?"

"Well, it'd be easier going up than climbing down at this point," I replied.

Three days later, Barry Rugo soloed *Open Cockpit*. He knew nothing of my undertaking and thought he'd bagged the first solo. His inspired ascent produced an ironic situation.

The heat was on: two down and one to go. *Open Cockpit* had been somewhat spontaneous; *Supercrack* was totally premeditated.

Dick was home. My headlights flashed against his car as I pulled into the driveway. It dawned on me that this was the end of the summer. Tomorrow would be my last day in the Gunks before classes started. Tomorrow would be it.

I had been house-sitting in New Paltz for Dick Williams and Rosie Andrews while they vacationed in Britain. Exceptionally fine August weather allowed for daily rituals of pulling, pumping and tweaking on solid quartzite. The result was a confidence that only comes from familiarity. Once my attention turned to school, the spell would be broken.

I greeted Dick in the living room and we talked about his trip. My attention was only partially on the conversation. Whisks of tomorrow's plan swept through my head and I felt like a kid with a secret.

Dick went to bed and I slouched down on the couch, draping my bag loosely over me. The night was warm, the insects noisy. I closed my eyes

Soloing is a rarely photographed private pursuit; however, Adele Hammond came along at the right time to snap this shot of Russ Clune starting up Open Cockpit.
PHOTO BY ADELE HAMMOND/CLUNE COLLECTION

and saw *Supercrack* in front of me. I envisioned my hands and feet on each move until I stood on top. Back at the base, I climbed it again. Perfect. Again. Perfect. Again.

The aroma of coffee filled the house at an obscenely early hour. Dick, unable to sleep because of jet lag, joined me for a cup as we exchanged good-byes. He thought I was headed directly home. I knew better. My truck puttered uphill toward the Trapps. I parked, pulled my bike out of the back, strapped my pack to my back and turned on the Walkman. Cool air rushed against my face as The Smiths blared through the headphones:

"All men have secrets and here is mine, so let it be known!"

I pedaled fast toward Skytop. At the base of *Supercrack* I was sweating and breathing hard from the ride. The crack looked long. I pictured myself on it, watched myself climb it from the perspective of an observer. Then I mentally climbed it as the climber, watching my feet and hands on each hold.

My breathing slowed down. Now the climb looked short. I liked that. My Walkman was off, but The Smiths still swirled in my head. I pulled my shoes on and laced them with the care of a diamond cutter, letting each toe find its favorite indentation before locking it into place. I squeezed my full chalk bag a few times, breaking the chunks down to the right consistency. I started up, went several moves and came down. The Smiths sang in my head:

"Ohhh, what difference does it make?"

Answer: Enough that I had to erase every iota of doubt. I went back to my pack and pulled out a rope and a couple of units. I climbed around the back of the pinnacle and anchored the toprope. At the bottom, I rigged a jumar to my harness for a self-belay.

I shot up the crack. It felt good and secure; just right. I dropped the rope and pulled the anchors. Back at the base, I sat and rubbed the soles of my shoes clean.

Automatic pilot switched on. The crack had the feel of a well-worn glove, every rugosity clicking into place. Footholds appeared with acute clarity, looking overly large. Thumb pinch with the right, index finger down with the left, feet stemmed, butterfly jam with the right, right foot pebble, left foot edge.

Internal dialogue made an uninvited appearance when my left hand clutched the jug above the roof. "What the hell are you doing?!" it exclaimed. I squashed the thought like a troublesome insect, and with a surge of adrenaline laybacked to the stance. A wave of relief washed over me. I chalked each hand thoroughly and continued up on steel-solid locks. On top I looked out over the valley toward town. My heart thumped audibly and a shudder ran the length of my body. Internal dialogue returned with two thoughts: "God, I love this place," and, "I'm retired."

Oh, the devil will find work for idle hands to do.

I met Jimmy Surette in North Conway the next day. At the time, Jim was a talented 17-year-old climber with a bright future. He glowed in delight when I told him about *Supercrack*.

"Wow, awesome!" he said. "I'm really glad you did that."

We went to the *Airation* buttress on Cathedral Ledge for the day's climbing. Jimmy silently put his shoes on. Next thing I knew he was soloing *Airation*, a 40-foot 5.11 finger crack. I watched in concern, but he had it in control. A few words of encouragement were all I gave.

Even as I worried, the competitive streak in me said, "Go for it." I squelched it. I realized my following would only spur him on. We had a talk when he came back down.

"Good job, man."

"Thanks."

"Listen, I don't want to sound like your old man, but it concerns me you did that right after I told you about *Supercrack*."

I told him that soloing was great, but asked him to keep it in perspective.

"Don't do it to impress anyone but yourself, it's not a shortcut to grandeur. It's a shortcut to nowhere."

Jimmy listened, then assured me it was no problem. He'd been wanting to do *Airation* for a while. I felt responsible, but could hardly say much more, being the pot calling the kettle black. I remembered "Noddy," a British climber, a Moffat groupie, who decided that soloing was the hot ticket to fame. It wasn't. John Kirk wrote in Noddy's obit: "He will never be famous. He was the guy who held Jerry Moffat's ropes. Another life finished before it had really begun."

As people started hearing about *Supercrack*, the compliments and congratulations flowed thick and fast. It bothered me a little then and still does. What I did was not glorious, was no amazing feat of derring-do. I had the thing wired into submission. It was simply the proper state of mind.

About a month later, I was at *Supercrack*. Todd Skinner had just led it and offered a toprope. I thought about what it would be like to fall off it. Last time I was here, falling had never entered my head.

I tied in and started up. The butterfly jam popped out; I was off, and everybody screamed.

I'm definitely retired.

I think.

KUMBHAKARNA—MY WAY

by Tomo Cesen

*B*orn in the Yugoslav Julian Alps in 1960, Tomo Cesen burst onto the
*international climbing scene with his winter trilogy of the three great
north faces of the Alps: the Eiger, Matterhorn and Grandes Jorasses. These
were followed by remarkable ascents in the Himalaya and Karakoram ranges,
highlighted by new routes up the north face of Yalung Kang (27,903 feet, also
known as Kanchenjunga West, a sub-summit of Kanchenjunga, the world's third
highest peak), a solo ascent of Broad Peak (26,402 feet), and a solo attempt on
the south spur of K2 (28,250 feet). These climbs foreshadowed perhaps the biggest
controversy in the history of mountaineering: Cesen's claimed first solo ascent
of what was at the time coined The Last Great Problem in the Himalaya—the
massive, 12,000-foot south face of Lhotse.*

*Rising 27,893 feet above sea level, Lhotse is the fourth highest peak in the
world, and in 1990 it was no secret among climbers that whoever managed to
do the first ascent of the south face—by any means—would gain instant notoriety
and make history, and probably earn the sponsorship needed to turn the pursuit
of big peaks into a full-time job. Then Tomo Cesen claimed the solo first ascent in
the spring of 1990, and the climbing world was turned on its head. Many great
climbers had died vying for this prize, and if Cesen's claim of a solo first ascent
(in an incredible 62-hour round trip from Base Camp) was true, it would
essentially cast all climbers as amateurs next to him.*

*The rumble of dissension started in the bars of Chamonix and spread like fire
through the European climbing community and press. How could Cesen be so
fit, so strong, so unbelievably skilled as to solo an unclimbed 12,000-foot wall
that had defeated teams of the world's best alpinists? When evidence surfaced
that seemed to dispute Cesen's claim, the doubts grew stronger and the rumbling*

louder. Finally, after exhaustive investigation, climber and author Greg Child wrote an article for Climbing magazine in which he provided strong arguments that some, if not all, of Cesen's solo Himalayan climbs were hoaxes—including the one related in the following story, a solo ascent of Kumbhakarna (formerly known as Jannu). Much of the controversy focused on the fact that Cesen lacked photographic evidence and/or witnesses for his most extreme climbs, and his accounts of the climbs were often vague and inconsistent. Despite this, many stuck up for Cesen as an incredible climber—the best in the world—and a man of impeccable character. By the time Child wrote his article in 1994, a controversy-weary Cesen told him that after months of battling the press and other climbers, he simply didn't really care anymore. "If people don't believe me," he said, "that's their problem." Child surmised that the only way to know for sure whether Cesen was telling the truth would be to climb the south face of Lhotse and look for the pitons Cesen claimed to have left near the top—"and I'll be damned if I'm going to do that," Child concluded.

At the root of this controversy—and others that have arisen throughout the history of mountaineering—is the fact that the line between the possible and impossible is somewhat fluid for the most extreme climbers. In a thousand different ways—and often knowing it only in hindsight—most extreme climbers are looking for an ascent to show them one true thing about life or about themselves. If any of Cesen's great climbs are conspicuous frauds, then the fluid line between possible and impossible has sadly, for Tomo Cesen, bled into the business of true and false, desire and reality. This would mean that even the most quintessential trial by fire—soloing cutting-edge world-class climbs—can lead one man just as far into illusion as it might lead another into the clean air of truth. And once that fluid line is passed over, retreat from either camp seems unlikely. If, on the other hand, Cesen is being truthful, then he has been the victim of a tragic and misguided effort to discredit him. Though dismal and ugly, this conclusion confirms the fundamental law of all climbing: nothing is guaranteed.

‡   ‡   ‡

For a year, I debated whether to try to climb Kumbhakarna solo. At one time, I spent an entire fortnight thinking of nothing else. After all, its direct north face was considered one of the most difficult in the world. Today, of course, I am delighted that I eventually went and I do not regret my decision to climb the face alone.

The north face of Kumbhakarna was first reconnoitered by New Zealanders in 1975. (At that time, the peak was known by climbers as Jannu, although it appears that the name has no local usage. The present official name—Kumbhakarna—is used throughout this article.) In 1982, a strong French team headed by Pierre Beghin spent two months on the face, eventually climbing the northeast ridge, but not climbing to the summit. In his account in the *American Alpine Journal*, 1983, Beghin states, "It was the most moving experience I'd ever had in the Himalaya because of the harshness of the wall. None of us had ever seen such a cold, steep face. The last 3,000 feet were like the Cima Ovest's north face in the Dolomites with much of the last 1,500 feet overhanging. When we discovered how smooth this part of the face was, we headed for the northeast ridge." The latter route was eventually climbed by the Japanese in 1986. This Japanese route was ascended again in October 1987, first by the Dutch—two of whom were killed on the descent—then by Frenchmen Beghin and Brik Decamp.

During the months prior to leaving for Kumbhakarna, taxing solo winter ascents of the *Pilier Rouge* on Mont Blanc, the north faces of the Eiger, the Matterhorn and the Grandes Jorasses and the south face of the Marmolada, convinced me that I was psychologically strong enough for a solo ascent among the Himalayan giants. These successes helped keep my mind off Kumbhakarna. But from the moment I packed my equipment two days before my departure, like it or not, my thoughts always dwelt on the climb.

Dr. Jan Kokalj, who accompanied me to the mountain almost by chance, was a good companion. Along with the liaison officer and Chindi, the cook, who also served as sirdar, we made a great team. We established Base Camp on April 22 at 4,600 meters at the edge of the Kumbhakarna Glacier. The following day and for several days after, Jan and I went to the foot of the face and anywhere else that afforded a good vantage. This was also essential for acclimatization. The upper part of the north face was clearly visible from Base Camp, but the lower part presented a puzzle which I needed to solve as soon as possible. The beginning of the route did not look encouraging. The face started with an icefall, which from our side of the glacier looked like heaped-up ice cubes, threatening to tumble down at any moment. But I was even more concerned by Kumbhakarna's upper face, composed of ice gullies and a smooth overhanging granite wall, all interspersed with giant roofs. A fantastic sight! The vague strategy I'd trekked in with needed thoughtful revision, especially in regards to the upper face. Before leaving home, I knew I could not plan an exact route. Although the threat of huge avalanches and falling seracs was not unacceptably great, whistling rocks and blocks of ice were proof that the face was lethal. Most of this mortar fire ended in the funnel at the bottom of the main wall. Clearly, I'd have to speed over that part of the climb in the still of night when, hopefully, the face was frozen solid.

April 27 dawned cloudy. During lunch, the sun's rays eventually pierced the clouds. How quickly one's mood can change! Chindi was a master of his craft. I decided to take along some of his cheese custards as well as crackers, tins of fish and drinks. Early that afternoon I left with Jan, who accompanied me to the start of the glacier. My fantastic mood matched the weather.

Alone on the glacier, I felt exhilarated—a good sign—and was in complete control of my feelings. I hung pitons and a spare ice-axe blade on my harness, put crampons on my feet and an ice axe in each hand. I had a rope and, of course, a helmet. My rucksack contained only spare clothing—gloves, glasses, food, drink, a sleeping bag and a bivouac sack. Not much gear to climb the nearly 10,000-foot-high north face of Kumbhakarna—it would be a great challenge.

After 200 meters of steep terrain I came to the first 10-meter-high stretch of vertical ice. Four hours later, at dusk, the lower part of the face was behind me and I rested for ten minutes. The valley below was already dark, but up here I could see satisfactorily despite the late hour. I climbed into the night, thankful that the falling rock and ice were easing off. Climbing this section in the day would have been suicide, but the night represented safety. There were 200 meters, perhaps a little more, of cramponing up a 70- to 80-degree couloir, topped by some difficult rock.

The new day broke when I reached the top of the icefield. I had to make a right turn to the next icefield, which was separated from the last one by the first really problematic part of the route. Very steep ice and granite slabs alternated. I oriented myself on the seracs at the beginning of the middle icefield. There was no possibility for protection in the crackless rock. I was glad to reach the top of the steep ice gully that led to the less steep icefield below some huge seracs. I rested.

A short rock step separated me from the final part of the face. Ice, rock, more ice, always followed by granite slabs. The exit from this section was spectacular. A gently sloping slab blocked the way to the last icefield before the vertical exit from the face. At sea level, without crampons and gloves, this might have been easy, but here it was quite a different matter. I couldn't remove my crampons, and plastic double boots are the last choice for delicate friction climbing. I grimly started up, my hands on the slab and my crampons in the thin ice below. I clawed with an ice axe at some small ice crystals. I felt enormous relief when my axe at last hit solid ice. This section was definitely not for the faint-hearted!

What was ahead, though, deserves a particular description. The face above 7,000 meters (22,965 feet) called for all my technique, but even more for psychological strength. I stared upward at an unbelievable scene. Only there, at 7,000 meters, did I realize what lay in store. There was no way back for me now. A vertical gully was filled with thin ice, sometimes interrupted by a few meters of rock. The rock appeared good, although it was clear that rock climbing with crampons would be very difficult. The feeling of uncertainty, which gives climbing a peculiar attraction and which I need from time to time, suddenly vanished. In these moments of utmost concentration, the world around you no longer exists. You have to stretch your capabilities and strength to the limit.

The nearly vertical slabs were covered with ice, no more than four inches thick. The consistently 80- to 90-degree slabs were on an average 30 to 40 meters high. I was dead tired and mentally exhausted. Due to the thin air, I couldn't climb without resting. But resting, hanging on a perilously placed axe, was too stressful. There were at least ten slabs. Several easier options existed, but none visible from below. I could only guess at the best route upward. On four occasions I used aid pitons, as the rock was too difficult to climb free with my crampons on. There was no safe place to remove my crampons. Fortunately, some cracks were wide enough for me to jam in a foot, relax my arms and get a short rest.

At the end of the rock, there was always ice again, hard, black, green, sometimes rotten, but almost always steep. Once I had to perform a pendulum; a narrow ice gully lost itself in unclimable granite. Vertical rock rose above, left and right. I noticed a tiny crack above me; I climbed almost to the top of the ice tongue, slowly and with great concern because the ice tongue threatened to snap off with each move. I hammered in a piton, threaded the rope, descended a little and swung to the side. Thus, I reached the continuation of the ice gully to the left.

Slowly, I was approaching the ridge, although there were extremely difficult sections right up to the crest. Suddenly I almost stumbled into the soft snow on the ridge. The summit of Kumbhakarna was very close, and the ridge leading to it presented no technical difficulties. I felt drained; I'd had enough of this kind of torture. I reached the summit just after 3:30 P.M., in deteriorating weather. To the south was a sea of gray clouds.

The usual afternoon worsening of weather would prevail that day too. For that reason, I wanted to descend the Japanese route as far as was possible. I had to rappel to reach the upper icefield of the Japanese route. Because the weather began to resemble a proper storm, there was no point in sitting it out in the middle of a 55- to 60-degree icefield. Heavy snowfall and strong cold winds forced me into a crevasse among the seracs.

The seemingly endless bivouac was marked by chattering teeth, quivering muscles, constantly checking my watch and hoping the last few days' weather pattern would prevail. With howling winds sweeping snowflakes in every direction through the fog and darkness, the bivouac seemed to never end. In the middle of the night, the storm finally abated. I continued down immediately, descending among the seracs for 100 meters. It was not the right way and led to a 15-meter-high vertical ice cliff. Not feeling like retracing my steps, I decided to rappel. At the edge of the serac I chiseled an ice mushroom with my ice axe and fixed the rope with a sling. Although this maneuver appears close to madness to the uninitiated, such an ice mushroom holds weight without danger.

The ice slopes leading to the lower seracs sometimes surprised me with black ice. During the day, I could have sought a better route, but in the darkness I descended the most direct line. Among the lower seracs I zigzagged left and right to stay among them for as long as possible. On the final section to the plateau I rappelled a few more times. The icefall in the jumbled mess of the Kumbhakarna Glacier was a mere formality. I chose a much easier route than for my ascent, albeit one a bit more dangerous. I told myself that if the seracs hadn't collapsed for a whole week, they'd last another hour or two.

Finally it was all over. When there is no more danger and the way ahead is easier, concentration falls. My walk across the glacier resembled the staggering of a drunk returning from a night out. Halfway to Base Camp Jan came toward me with a broad smile stretching across his face. It was wonderful to see another human, especially one who had kept his fingers crossed through my climb. It took five hours to reach Base Camp from the foot of the face; it would normally have taken two. I was exhausted, finished. After great effort over three days, all with very little food, my stomach was not prepared for a feast. Only liquids went down easily. That afternoon we drank a lot.

Some people thought that the north face of Kumbhakarna could not be solo climbed. I did not agree and felt that I would succeed. For me it is important that matters in which I believe so much must be resolved in my own way. And Kumbhakarna is only a part of what I believe in.

THE ONLY BLASPHEMY

by John Long

*W*ith well over 5,000 climbs, most in the 50- to 150-foot range, *Joshua Tree National Park (or simply Josh) remains one of the most popular winter rock climbing areas on earth. The rough-textured quartz monzonite affords superior friction and most every monolith is riddled with cracks — two factors that give the free soloer something to sink their hands into. Climbers from Spain to Greece, from Iran to Oklahoma all have soloing stories of hanging precariously from a grainy jam on a wind-swept dome, wondering how they ever climbed themselves into such a fix. The following is one such story.*

‡ ‡ ‡

At speeds beyond 80, the California cops jail you, so for the first twenty miles I kept it right around 79. Tobin used to drive 100 miles an hour, till his Datsun exploded in flames on the freeway out by Running Springs. After half an hour I was doing 90 mph. Josh came quickly, but the stark night dragged.

The morning sun peered over the flat horizon, gilding the rocks spotting the desert carpet. The biggest stones are little more than 150 feet high. Right after breakfast I ran into John Bachar, who at the time was probably the world's foremost free climber. He'd bounce around the country in his old VW van, hanging at whichever climbing area had the sunniest weather. All climbs were easy for Bachar, and he had to make his own difficulties. He completely dominated the cliff with his grace and confidence. He never rattled, never lost control, and you knew if he ever got killed climbing, it wouldn't be his fault. It would be a gross transgression proving climbing was foolish and all wrong. You'd sell all your gear and curse God for the rest of your life—on aesthetic, not moral grounds. Bachar had been out at Joshua Tree for about two months, and his free soloing feats astonished everyone.

Two weeks prior, a friend of mine had decked while free soloing at Joshua Tree. I later inspected the base of the route, wincing at the grisly blood stains, the tufts of matted hair. Free soloing is unforgiving, but okay, I thought. You just have to be realistic, not some dupe goaded by peer pressure or ego.

It was winter, and college checked my climbing to weekends, so my motivation was there, but my fitness was not. Straightaway, Bachar suggested a "Half Dome Day." Half Dome in Yosemite is 2,000 feet high, call it 20 rope lengths. Since at Joshua, there are no rocks even remotely as big as Half Dome, all of our climbs would be short ones, roughly 150 feet long. The notion was to climb 20 such routes, which would equate to 2,000 feet. That would give us our Half Dome Day.

In a wink, Bachar was booted up, cinching the sling on his chalk bag. "Ready?" Only then did I realize he intended to climb all 2,000 feet free solo, without a rope. To save face, I agreed, thinking, "Well, if he suggests something too crazy, I'll just draw the line." I felt jackals running up and down my spine, and kept reminding myself that I was the first one to start soloing at Josh, and had, in fact, introduced Bachar to the art several years before. But the jackals kept running.

We embarked on vertical rock; twisting feet and jamming hands into bulging cracks, smearing the toes of our skin-tight boots onto tenuous bumps, pulling over roofs on bulbous holds, palming off rough rock and marveling at it all. A little voice occasionally asked me just how good a flexing, quarter-inch hold could be. If you're solid, you set curled fingers or pointed toes on that quarter-incher and push or pull perfunctorily. And after the first few routes, I felt solid.

Our method remained the same: We'd climb a hard route up a particular formation—rarely above 150 feet—then descend via an easy route to save time and because downclimbing difficult rock solo is twice as hard and ten times as dangerous. After three hours, we'd disposed with a dozen climbs, and felt invincible. We upped the ante to a stiff 5.10—expert terrain. We slowed considerably, but by early afternoon, we'd climbed 20 pitches: the Half Dome day was history. As a finale, Bachar suggested we solo a 5.11—an exacting effort even for Bachar. Back then, some twenty years ago, 5.11 was serious business. There were a few 5.12s around, but not many. I hadn't climbed in several weeks and was exhausted from racing up twenty different climbs in about five hours, having survived the last four or five on rhythm and momentum alone. Regardless, I followed Bachar over to Intersection Rock, the "hang" for local climbers and the locale for this day's final solo.

He wasted no time, and scores of milling climbers—half of them Europeans—froze like statues when he started up. He moved with flawless precision, plugging his fingertips into shallow pockets in the 105-degree wall. I scrutinized his moves, making mental notes on the intricate sequence. He paused at 50 feet, directly beneath the crux bulge. Splaying his left foot out onto a slanting edge, he pinched a tiny rib and pulled through to a gigantic bucket hold. Then he walked up the last 100 feet of vertical rock like a kid climbing a staircase. From the summit, Bachar flashed down that sly, candid snicker, awaiting my reply.

I was booted up and covered in chalk, facing a notorious climb. Fifty impatient eyes gave me the once over, as if to say, "Well?" That little voice said, "No problem," and I believed it. I drew several deep breaths, if only to convince myself. I didn't consider the consequences, only the moves. I started up.

A body length of easy stuff, then those pockets, which I fingered adroitly before yarding with maximum might. The first bit passed quickly. Everything was clicking along, severe but steady, and I glided into the "coffin zone" (above 50 feet) faster than I could reckon. Then, as I splayed my foot out onto the slanting edge, the chilling realization came that, in my haste, I'd bungled the sequence, my hands were too low on the puny rib-hold and my power was going fast. My foot started vibrating and I was instantly desperate, wondering if and when my body would freeze and plummet. There was no reversing any of this because you can't downclimb truly hard rock any more than a hurdler can run the 110 "highs" backward. The only way off was up. A montage of black images flooded my brain.

I glanced between my legs and my gut churned at the thought of a free fall onto the boulders. The little voice bellowed, "Do something. Now." My breathing was frenzied while my arms, gassed from the previous 2,000 feet, felt like concrete. Pinching that little rib, I sucked my feet up so as to extend my arm and jam my hand into the bottoming crack above. But the crack was too shallow, and accepted but a third of my hand. I was stuck, terrified, my whole existence focused down to a pinpoint, a single move.

Shamefully, I understood the only blasphemy—to willfully jeopardize my life, which I had done, and it crucified me. I knew that wasted seconds could—then the world stopped, or was it preservation instinct kicking my brain into hypergear? In a heartbeat I'd realized my urgent desire to live. But my regrets could not alter my situation: arms shot, legs wobbling, head on fire. Then my fear overwhelmed itself, leaving me hollow and mortified. To concede, to let go and fall, would have been easy. The little voice calmly intoned, "At least die trying."

I punched my hand deeper into the bottoming crack. If only I could execute this one crux move, I'd get an incut jug-hold, could rest off it before the final section. I was afraid to eyeball my crimped hand, scarcely jammed in the shallow crack. It *had* to hold my 205 pounds, on an overhanging wall, with scant footholds, and this seemed ludicrous, impossible.

My body jittered there for minutes. My jammed hand said, "no way" but the little voice said, "Might as well try it . . ."

I pulled up slowly—my left foot still pasted to that sloping edge— and that big bucket-hold was right there. I almost had it. Got it! Simultaneously, my right hand ripped from the crack and my foot flew off the edge: all my weight hung from an enfeebled left arm. Adrenaline powered me atop the Thank God bucket where I pressed my chest to the wall, got that 205 pounds over my feet, and start shaking violently. I'd been hanged—in fact I'd hung myself—but somehow the rope had broken.

Ten minutes passed before I could press on. I would rather have yanked out my wisdom teeth with vice grips. Dancing black orbs dotted my vision as I clawed up the last 100 feet and onto the summit.

"Looked a little shaky," Bachar laughed, flashing that trademark snicker.

That night I drove into town and got a bottle. Sunday, while Bachar went for an El Cap day (3,000 feet, free solo, of course), I wandered listlessly through dark desert corridors, scouting for turtles, making garlands from wildflowers, relishing the skyscape—doing all those things a person does on borrowed time.

OUR MAN IN EVEREST: MAURICE WILSON SURFACES EVERY FEW YEARS, ONLY TO BE DUTIFULLY REBURIED

by Lawrence Millman

aurice Wilson knew nothing about mountaineering when he set out to scale Mount Everest alone, believing that he could prove Mallory and Irvine's demise was due to—of all things—the intake of food. Stubborn innocence and religious corruption led Wilson to buy a second-hand plane, somehow attain his wings and deposit himself on the Mother of All Mountains. His diary, which was eventually recovered, told little of his struggles to solo the highest peak in the land— but his dead body told it all. Maurice Wilson was not a man to be kept down. Or so is the ghastly message of Everest herself, who periodically trots out Wilson's corpse as a warning to other mountaineers. In the following piece, writer Lawrence Millman examines the curious case of Maurice Wilson, solo climber extraordinaire—or deluded nutcase.

‡   ‡   ‡

If Maurice Wilson had not existed, it's highly unlikely that a member of the scribbling trade would have thought to invent him. Instead, we'd beseech our Muses to come up with someone a little less outrageous, like, for example, Sir Edmund Hillary. But Maurice Wilson did exist; and strange to say, he continues to exist, a testimony, of sorts, to the human spirit.

55

Born in Bradford, Yorkshire, in 1898, the son of a well-to-do woolens manufacturer, Maurice seemed headed for the same kind of stolid career as Hillary when the Great War intervened. The young man fought at Ypres and was much decorated. Much traumatized too. After the war he suffered fatigue, depression, inexplicable aches and pains. No doctor could help, so he turned to a homeopath, a man with decidedly Eastern whims. Food's the problem, always is, he informed Maurice. Food's bad for a person's body. Just fast for a couple of weeks, old chap, and you'll be as good as new. Maurice had nothing to lose, so he subsisted for thirty-five days on a diet of rice water, with a few slugs of meditation thrown in. And lo! by the thirty-fifth day he indeed seemed to be, if not as good as new, at least healthier than he'd been in a long time. Shortly thereafter he had a vision in which an unusually thin but otherwise robust God appeared to him. The Supreme Being was taking the cure too!

From then on Maurice set himself the task of bringing this cure before the eyes of the world. One day he happened on a newspaper cutting about the ill-fated 1924 Everest expedition. He read it through with interest, deciding that if Mallory and Irvine had only fasted they would have reached the hitherto unreachable summit of Everest, lived to tell the tale and been able to forgo the hateful task of high-altitude cooking. Thus he concocted a plan for his own personal Everest expedition. He would fly solo to the mountain, crash his plane on the East Rongbuk Glacier, and—dosing himself with rice water—trot up to the summit, Union Jack in hand.

There were two practical objections to Maurice's plan. He knew nothing about mountain climbing and he couldn't fly a plane. Mere details. He bought a second-hand Gipsy Moth, rechristened it *Ever Wrest*, and proceeded to take flying lessons at the London Aero Club. That he earned his pilot's license is indicative of the loose, if not downright unfettered, standards of the time. As for climbing, he made a few modest scrambles in Snowdonia and pronounced himself fit. The prospect of altitude sickness didn't trouble him, for he reasoned that the less food his body took in, the more room it'd have for oxygen, a commodity he knew to be rather more scarce on Everest than in North Wales.

By April 1933 he was ready to gate crash the mountain Tibetans call Chomolugma, the Mother Goddess of the Earth. But first he decided to say good-bye to his parents. En route to Bradford his engine cut out and he crashed into a farmer's hedgerow. He was unhurt. Undaunted too. A month later he was ready to try again. But by now the Air Ministry had caught wind of his eccentric plan and sent him a restraining order in the form of a telegram. Ignoring this, off he flew. Somehow *Ever Wrest* managed to splutter and wheeze passage as far as Darjeeling, India, but there it was impounded. Well, I'll just have to walk the rest of the distance, Maurice announced. The British refused him permission to enter Tibet on foot, whereupon our resourceful traveler simply disguised himself as a Sherpa and, as promised, walked the rest of the distance.

On April 12, 1934, Maurice reached the Rongbuk Monastery. Two days later he set off by himself to ascend the Mother Goddess of the Earth. His most important item of gear was a shaving mirror. This he intended to use as a heliograph from the summit, so the world would know of his success. With an ice axe borrowed from the head lama, he began hacking steps, none of which led in the direction of the summit. At one point he found some discarded crampons, but such was his ignorance—nay, innocence—that he just threw them away, having no idea what they were for. His haphazard ascent was finally brought to a halt by whiteout conditions. In his diary he wrote: "No use going any further. It's the weather that has beaten me—what damned bad luck!"

Back at the monastery he engaged the services of two local Sherpas, Rinzing and Tewang, for another assault on the mountain. They'd show him the proper route to the summit, and then he'd be able to carry on by himself.

So it was that the slightly revised Maurice Wilson Everest Expedition made the ascent to Camp 3. Here they discovered a food cache left behind by Hugh Ruttledge's expedition the previous year, and Maurice—late of the rice water persuasion—happily gorged himself on anchovy paste, Ovaltine, sardines, King George chocolates, and other goodies from Fortnum & Mason's. One can imagine the erstwhile faster turning to his Sherpas and guiltily pressing a chocolate-smudged finger to his lips.

For the next three days a ferocious blizzard pinned the party to their tents even as it threatened to launch those tents all the way into China. Then, on May 21, the blowing abruptly ceased. Rinzing and Maurice started up toward the site of Camp 4, not trotting, hardly even climbing, but mostly clawing at the iced up mountain. Naive Maurice queried his companion as to the whereabouts of the ice steps Ruttledge had made the previous year. They'd found his chocolates, hadn't they?

Around noon they parted: Rinzing went back to Camp 3 while Maurice climbed on by himself. In the next few days he distinguished himself by starting an avalanche and sliding backward down 200 feet of verglas, breaking some ribs. When at last he staggered back to camp, he was considerably more dead than alive. But defeated? Not bloody likely. He'd just come back to pick up his Sherpas, who, he figured, might be of some use in his assault on Camp 4. But the Sherpas refused to climb even another fifty feet with him, for they'd come to the conclusion that their sahib was, at the very least, cracked right down the middle.

So it ended for Maurice Wilson exactly where it began: a man alone against the mountain. No fellow climbers, no superfluous technology. No rice water, either. *Alone*. The most stubborn Yorkshireman in the world against the most stubborn mountain in the world. Now we watch that man trudging wearily through the snow. Now he stands at the foot of the North Col and gazes up, up, up . . .

The following year Eric Shipton, Charles Warren and H.W. Tilman were themselves trying to reconnoiter a North Col route to the summit. It was the morning of July 9 and Warren was walking a little ahead of the others. A few hundred yards above Camp 3 he spotted a perfectly good pair of boots lying in the snow. Soon he saw a crumpled green tent torn from its guylines, along with an equally crumpled Union Jack. He thought this might be an earlier expedition's dumpsite until he saw the body itself, huddled in the snow. "I say," he called out to Shipton, "it's that fellow Wilson."

According to Warren, Maurice was wearing a mauve pullover, light-weight flannel trousers, and thin socks, attire more suitable for high tea in Mayfair than the high elevations of the Himalayas. But in the next few years another story spread: Maurice had been dressed in ladies' underwear. Though this story has never been verified, a woman's high-heeled shoe was found close to Camp 3 by a later expedition. Whatever Maurice's sartorial preference, it was clear that death had come about by exposure, not starvation. Which, one feels, is how this devotee of starvation would have preferred it.

Near the body Shipton located the weather-beaten diary in whose pages Maurice had recorded his perpetual struggle with the mountain. The entries were nearly all of a piece. "No food, no water . . . terrible cold . . . dead tired . . . must somehow go on . . ." But of how he occupied himself toward the end, or roughly when that end might have come, the diary provides no clue.

Shipton and Warren wrapped the body in the tent and slid it into a nearby crevasse, where, by all rights, it should have remained. But you can't keep a good man down. Over the years Maurice has surfaced with macabre regularity, thrust forth by the movements of the glacier. In 1960

Chinese climbers found him and dutifully reburied him. More recently, he's been sighted by Japanese, German and yet more Chinese mountaineers. It's as if the Mother Goddess were offering her myriad visitors advice by repeatedly putting Maurice on display, as if she were telling them: Dance to the beat of your own drummer, my friends. Follow your star wherever it may lead you. And above all, keep the faith, as this gentleman himself seems to have kept it, even unto his own very cold end.

The last entry in Maurice's diary, penciled thinly but clearly, in a shaky hand reads: "Off again, gorgeous day . . ."

ALONE ON THE NORTH FACE
OF ALBERTA

by Mark Wilford

*M*ark Wilford began as a talented rock climber, earning himself a reputation as somewhat of a wild man owing to a bold streak wide as the Khumbu Icefall. When Wilford transitioned into alpine climbing in the early '80s, many of his rock climbing friends thought it wouldn't be long before the Almighty would draw this rambunctious Colorado climber back to the Promised Land. However, several grim solo climbs, including the north face of the Eiger, proved to friends that Wilford's judgment and sense of self-preservation were in fact on par with his technical skills. All these things would be put to the test when Wilford set off to try and solo the north face of Mount Alberta, a remarkable achievement featured in the following story. Ironically, another legendary American climber—Tobin Sorenson, who was cut from the same bold cloth as Wilford—perished a decade earlier while attempting to solo Alberta's great north face.

‡   ‡   ‡

Inspiration to climb Mount Alberta came early in my climbing career via a photo spread by Jim Stuart in the 1973 *Ascent*, entitled "Canada in Winter." A two-page photo of Alberta's north face, plastered in snow and ice and looking very sinister, held my attention. Only a few pages farther into the issue was George Lowe's account of his and Jock Glidden's first ascent of this great north face. Even more unfathomable than the face was how anyone could climb it. It was a long time before I would fully un-

Intimidation, Canadian-Rockies style, comes in the form of the northeast ridge and north face of Mount Alberta. PHOTO BY MARK WILFORD

derstand the remoteness and grandeur of this great peak and the significance of their climb.

This *Ascent* received only brief perusal over the years. It wasn't until 1989 that I pulled out the journal with intent. Business would take me to the Rockies the following January. I wanted a project for my visit.

Ignorance and arrogance reared their big heads. I managed to have a tremendous epic on the trip, but failed to muster more than hot air as far as Alberta was concerned. I limped back home, embarrassed by my brashness, and attempted to extricate my tail from between my legs with proclamations of returning.

My pride had mended and my head had swollen sufficiently by the summer of 1990, so that I was ready for round two.

After the marathon drive from Colorado, I managed the morale-eating approach fording glacial rivers and groveling up thousands of feet of scree to the top of Woolley Shoulder. I finally confronted the source of my desire. The remoteness and magnificence of this vision would be worth the outcome. The mountain loomed above a sea of glaciers and vastness. Spent from the day's march, I made my way to the tiny hut.

The following day I rested, then took an afternoon stroll to the base of Alberta's northeast ridge. I got a close look at the north face, as intimate as most would want to get with this widowmaker. Close to my conscience was the memory of Tobin Sorenson's fatal attempt to solo the face ten years earlier. Tobin's reputation was so strong that it had courted immortality; yet here was the stage for his last act. The reality of it all was sobering. The valve retaining my motivation leaked a bit.

Because of easier terrain and less chance of rockfall, my intentions were for the northeast ridge. Ease of access also played a role in this choice. With my blinders on, I set to work on the steep black limestone of the ridge.

Over a period of a few hours I tensioned and free climbed my way up 200 overhanging feet—solid, but almost crackless, save for a few knifeblade placements. I fixed lines and scurried back to the hut. Smug in my tiny amount of success, I wrapped myself tightly in a shroud of ignorance and struggled for sleep.

I set out the next morning and quickly topped the fixed ropes. Above, I cruised an easy icefield and then hit the ridge crest. From there, the mountain began showing its soul. The facade of beauty and charm was peeled away with each step. Actually, part of the mountain was physically peeled away with each step. The black tile gave way to a putrid yellow shale—only gravity held the stacked dinner plates in their precarious position. I felt like a drunk stumbling through an antique store tightly packed with china and glass—while a neon sign flashes "You break it, you buy it." I wove my way around little towers of teetering plates, all too aware of the voids growing on my left and right—1,200 feet down the east face and 2,000 feet down the north face. After navigating what seemed like miles of tightwire, I came to a small spire in a horizontal section of the ridge. It stood there like a sentinel—not so much guarding the mountain from me, but rather questioning my purpose, searching my soul for logic and sanity. Leaning next to it, I could gaze over into the darkness of the north face. A 2,000-foot ice tongue dropped steeply away from the gangrenous yellow bands. I could hear Tobin's whispers drifting over to me. I craned my neck to catch the words, but couldn't. I sucked in air to calm my stomach.

It was still early in the day, and I'd been making steady progress. As I gazed at the north face, I felt a lurid sensation. Perched out of sight, I was a voyeur watching the maiden undress. My eyes would burn if I didn't turn away.

The Sentinel put it to me again, "What do you want?" I passed on with a dread, knowing I had no answer to the question, and reached the steep, black limestone of the headwall.

I was leery of the apparent solidity of the black rock. Traversing the yellow band had spawned a monster of dread in my stomach and seriously undermined my faith. I pondered my inability to answer the Sentinel's question. What was my purpose? Voices drifted up to me, some from across the north face, others from the east—voices of men and of women. My confidence was being devoured by these dervishes. I set some dubious anchors and started up the headwall. After some reasonable face climbing, I came up under a black roof. I placed some pro in a sharp crack and then moved out left and up over the bulge. The moves were cool, the rock okay, but my psych had been bled so low that each reach became a major effort. It was like pulling against a huge rubber band—straining harder and harder, waiting for the snap to end it all. I made it over the bulge onto decent rock, but was unable to trust it. No more pro for quite a ways . . .

I looked 3,000 feet down into the darkness of the north face. The void held my gaze and slowly sucked out my remaining nerve. Voices again—some from home, some from strangers—beckoned me down. I faced the torment of retreat and failure. I backed down the overhanging moves, down to the belay. I swallowed hard, almost gagging. My eyes watered. The climbing wasn't too hard, or the temperature too cold; it wasn't the lack of gear that stopped me. The climbing was merely too scary. I wanted my life—that was my answer to the Sentinel.

It was a long, long way down.

For the next twelve months I agonized over my relationship with Alberta. I had little choice. The experience had scored a vivid imprint into my mind. I couldn't escape the mountain easily, even though I was back home in Colorado. My copy of *Ascent* remained accessible whenever my desire welled up. It became obvious that another round with the mountain was inevitable.

In August 1991, I loaded the trusty wagon up for another blast north. The strings of home were painfully tight this time. Breaking them to venture on this journey took immense determination and understanding. Enduring 1,200 miles of white-line fever at 80 to 90 miles per hour, I blasted past Banff and up to the Columbia Icefields Parkway.

I was back.

It was an ugly reception. Rain pounded down and the campsites were full. I waded through the mud trying to stretch out my road-warped back. What the hell was I doing here again? I felt alone already; my purpose was a distant memory. I was thinking of easier objectives as I climbed back into the wagon. I didn't make it far up the road before the rain abated and a beam of sunshine broke through the black clouds. I stopped and reveled in the sun.

My psych fired up again. I pulled out my gear and began the pacifying task of sharpening my ice tools until the late Canadian sun set.

I awoke the next morning to partly cloudy skies—better than rain, but not what I was banking on.

"You should have been here last week—best weather all summer." The rangers gave me this classic line as I signed in. Objective: Mount Alberta north face. Number in party: One. Estimated return: I hope.

Previous experience lent its hand in loading my pack. Less of this and that, more of these and those. I made one last phone call home, sharing concerns and assurances of care. The wagon motored me down to the river crossing and I climbed out. Good-bye, old buddy—keep a cold one ready for me.

I donned my Tevas and started to forge the frigid Sunwapta River.

The long march hadn't gotten any shorter and Woolley Shoulder was still a bitch, but somehow it all seemed to go by pretty fast. That afternoon I was back at the cozy hut. Not alone, either. Two fellows from Boulder were on their way out after a week of pondering the north face— too much rockfall. It was nasty, windy, and wet that night. I was relieved; no better excuse to bail than bad weather.

The next morning my friends left, and I lay about in a quagmire of indecision. Finally, I hiked to the north face overlook. The weather had cleared, taking with it my main excuse for backing out. I was committed now.

I didn't spend much time at the overlook—I knew the powers of the north face and how it could drain my psych. Back at the hut that night, I was tormented by nightmares of all sorts and I prayed for bad weather. It didn't come.

The next morning, the sky was clear and so I fulfilled my commitment. After a quick rappel and some downclimbing, I arrived on the glacier below the wall. The snow was dirty and pitted with rockfall. The air temperature was above freezing. I scoped the face and wondered where I would breach the headwall 2,500 feet up.

The initial 2,000-foot icefield looked straightforward, almost casual. I wandered over to the obvious break in the bergschrund to access the wall. It was apparent that the rocks littering the glacier's surface were recent projectiles from above. At the schrund I donned my crampons and, with little ceremony, ventured into the lair of the face.

I moved up and left on slabs toward the massive ice ramp. Once there, I realized I could climb just as easily on the adjacent rock slabs. I gained attitude quickly, until increasing steepness forced me onto the ice.

Until then, I had been somewhat protected from rockfall. This changed as I moved onto the ice. The warm temperatures freed numerous rocks that had been tethered by the night's frost. Initially, the main barrage was to my left. But as I moved higher, I became more exposed and the rockfall hit closer.

I quickened my pace, launching myself into the gauntlet. My lungs burned, and dry heat scorched my throat. The flame flickered down to my calves, licking the life out of them. There was no time or place to rest. A rock the size of a half-gallon milk-carton hurled just past my head. The clattering of high-speed missiles sounded like a fleet of helicopters. I was traveling through a corridor of terror.

I aimed for the nearest buttress of yellow rock. By now my body had taken charge, while my electrified brain drank in the surging adrenaline. My pace forced me to take brief intermissions from the horror show. Finally I arrived at the sanctuary of the yellow buttress, where I regrouped, set some dubious anchors and fueled up.

It was this section of shattered yellow shale from which Tobin Sorenson fell to his death, as indicated by rock embedded in the pitons found with his rope. With Tobin in mind, I cautiously worked my way up and through the rotten band. After 300 feet I came to a band of shattered black tile.

Anchors were becoming increasingly difficult to place. Any crack larger than a hairline usually indicated that the surrounding rock was loose. My belay anchors were now combinations of knifeblades.

I was gaining on the headwall but beginning to lose my perspective of the route above. Upon reaching the toe of the headwall I had little idea of where the Lowe route had gone. The only sign of previous activity was a single yellow sling 100 feet above. This wasn't convincing evidence, so I traversed a full rope-length to my left, then one to my right, searching for an alternate route. None of the potential lines I saw were convincing either; I returned to my belay and proceeded to climb to the tattered sling. It seemed to have been used for retreat. Nonetheless, I pushed through for one more pitch.

The climbing was vertical and overhanging. Fortunately, the quality of rock improved, but I still encountered numerous loose blocks. Eventually the crack system I was following petered out, and I was forced to descend from the headwall.

The hour was growing late and I decided it best to secure a bivouac. From the headwall I made two diagonal rappels to the east, back onto the yellow band. After a little more traversing, I found a suitable ledge. My position and commitment on the wall were just beginning to sink in.

I still wasn't sure how to proceed through the headwall, yet when I peered down the sweeping icefield below, retreat seemed equally improbable. I felt as though I was in a labyrinth.

Spent from the day's efforts, my mind was given a reprieve as I sank into a healthy sleep. That night the weather moved in and frosted me with a light snow.

In the morning, my position hadn't changed, but rest had given me new strength to weigh my options. It was still not clear to me where the line up the headwall went. I was also certain that I didn't want to retreat down the icefield. As an alternative, I could make a long traverse left to the northeast ridge and, once there, continue on up or escape. This traverse, though, would require climbing and rappelling across the terrifying black tile.

After much deliberation, I began the traverse. Finding anchors (usually a single A4 knifeblade) and tensioning/rappelling diagonally across the shale was a tedious process. I'd climb up as high as possible before I pulled the ropes. This process kept me from losing any elevation along the traverse. It was, needless to say, a most frightening series of maneuvers.

After a brief eternity, I finally reached the sun-bathed towers on the

With the void tugging at his heels and nothing to stop him if he falls, Mark Wilford maintains control of his nerves enough to arrange a photo of himself on the north face of Mount Alberta. PHOTO BY MARK WILFORD

northeast ridge. Ironically, I had arrived at precisely the point from which I'd retreated one year earlier. I felt a strange familiarity—mixing fear from the year before with the sun's warm comfort.

I was once again faced with a difficult decision—the same one I'd faced a year ago, when I'd opted out. I knew now that I'd never return to this place. I also knew that the ridge above had been done, and that retreat, though involved, would be possible.

The climbing above was steep, yet on relatively solid rock, which I accepted this time rather than suspected. I was able to move quickly, free climbing every pitch, self-belayed to provide an element of safety. In places, the route overhung and demanded crack climbing up to 5.10.

After eight pitches, the angle decreased and I moved into some steep gullies. A fixed pin indicated earlier passage. I became very tired and dehydrated. To save weight, I had no stove—the only moisture I consumed all day was from sucking meltwater from the rocks. A couple hundred feet higher, I encountered steep, unconsolidated snow on the east edge of the ridge.

At one point I came upon a single bolt on a small island of rock in a sea of crappy snow—a sign of desperation from an earlier ascent. My ropes were coiled, and the bolt was of no use to me. I tiptoed along the sharp ridge, leery of the rotten snow on my left and the shattered rock perched above the void on my right.

It was time to stop before exhaustion forced a mistake. After clearing a small perch, I began to collect some drips from a serac. The view was awesome. From my bivy I could look 4000 feet straight down the north face. To the southeast was the monstrous north face of the North Twin. To the south and west I could see an endless ocean of mountain peaks. I settled in for a long peaceful night.

Once again dawn found me dusted with snow and submerged in a whiteout. Still tired, but in grip of my faculties, I packed and balanced up the thin, steep snow ridge above. A large cornice formed on my left, and I was forced to drop down onto the north edge of the ridge. The abyss licked at my boots.

Higher up, crevasses intersected the cornice, offering obstacle upon obstacle. Finally, the angle declined and a few yards farther I found myself on the summit platform. As if choreographed, the clouds parted, allowing views of the Athabasca River Valley far below. I spent little time in celebration, for the weather was still threatening and the long descent down the *Japanese Route* awaited. A half-mile of ridge scrambling and a dozen rappels later I was finally out of Alberta's grasp.

KANCHENJUNGA SOLO

by Pierre Beghin

O nly Everest (29,028 feet) and K2 (28,250 feet) rise higher than Kanchenjunga (28,208 feet), whose main summit was first climbed in 1955 by Britons George Band and fabled rock climber Joe Brown. One of Nepal's most massive mountains, Kanchenjunga's three-mile-long summit ridge (consisting of Main, Central and South summits) is hammered by winds and monsoon snows, and its serac barriers regularly send down stupendous avalanches. Such is the mountain on which French climber Pierre Beghin made the first solo ascent in 1983, one of the outstanding mountaineering achievements of all time. In 1987, Beghin returned to the Kanchenjunga massif and, with fellow French climber Eric Decamp, made the audacious second ascent alpine style (continuous ascent with no fixed ropes to facilitate retreat) of the ridge leading to the south summit, know as Kumbhakarna (formally known as Jannu, 25,294 feet), the site of a controversy also addressed in this book. Pierre Beghin died in 1992 on Annapurna 1.

‡   ‡   ‡

On my return from Jannu November 1982, I obtained permission to climb Kanchenjunga's southwest face in the autumn of 1983. In March 1983 I decided on a solo ascent. Despite six years of Himalayan experience, the prospect was terrifying. Would I have the necessary determination to raise the funds, to organize the expedition and to carry it all out? My wife Annie was there to back me up. Along with three friends, she would accompany me to Base Camp. Without her support, I should have given it up and joined some other more reasonable project.

On August 28 we set out on the long approach with 35 porters, certainly the smallest expedition organized to climb Kanchenjunga. After eleven days of monsoon, crossing up and down steep terrain, we reached the last village, Yamplain. Porter tariffs jumped alarmingly. On the Yalung Glacier, three days from Base Camp, most of the men quit. With the seven who stayed, we shuttled, all of us carrying 65 pounds. Finally on September 17 we set up Base Camp on a promontory above the glacier at 17,400 feet. I had wondered if we'd ever get there!

Despite the unsettled monsoon weather, I set out alone. In three relays I carried 120 pounds of gear up the ridge to 20,000 feet. Each day I had to rebreak the trail. Beyond the ridge I fixed the route for 650 feet down the cliff, which gave access to Kanchenjunga's middle slopes. I had to reclimb this each time I descended to Base Camp. Camp 1 was set up on September 2 at 20,350 feet.

Next, the middle slopes: 3,250 feet of steep, complex terrain, crevasses alternating with seracs—a labyrinth. I had to make numerous detours to avoid crossing crevasses, the bugaboo of the solo climber. On September 29 I was on the upper plateau at 23,625 feet, where I pitched a second tent. The constant wind forced me to build a wall all around the tent lest it get blown straight off the mountain.

At the beginning of October, bad weather set in. I returned to Base Camp, where the waiting transformed me into a monster impossible to

Kanchenjunga, third highest mountain in the world. PHOTO: ANNIE BEGHIN/FOC PHOTO

be around. To escape the sinister atmosphere, Annie stayed with Tibetan shepherds in the Ramehe pastures.

Only on October 6 could I climb again. On the 8th I crossed the bergschrund of the 3,500-foot-high summit couloir and set up my tent at 25,275 feet.

At dawn on October 9, I set out for the summit; however, strong southwest winds soon drove clouds into the massif. I turned tail and began the long descent. I rushed to beat the fog to the crevassed zone—to be able to see my way through. After ten exhausting hours, I was back at Base Camp to wait out more bad weather.

On October 14 the sun shone again. I left for my second and doubtless last attempt. I couldn't stand much more solitude but I had invested too much effort to give up yet.

I spent the afternoon in front of my tent at Camp 1, observing the fantastic scene before and above me. I was struck by the absolute silence that reigns in these vast stretches of snow, up which the shadows of the clouds slowly crept from the valley. A strange feeling seized me as if the absence of noise indicated reprobation, an objection to my presence in this lifeless place. The least sound I made seemed to bring forth hostile glances. Behind that wall of silence, beyond the mountains that stretched out to the horizon, I felt a world from which I was excluded.

On October 16, at 25,275 feet, I prepared, like a medieval knight, for a "watch over my weapons." The icy west wind gusted; the cold bit to the bone. I tried to sleep, shifting in vain to find a relaxed position. Within the tiny tent I perceived a spirit at my side. All around me it was white, indistinct. Was I dreaming or awake? Was a spirit present or did I lack oxygen?

On October 17 at five o'clock, I leave my bivouac. My hands and feet soon are numb. Nonetheless, I progress. At 26,900 feet I leave the couloir and traverse steep snow and rock toward the summit. I have never felt so far distant from the land of the living. Wherever I look there is no indication of life. Yet 7,500 feet below me is a tent: Annie has set up her tent on a 20,000-foot ridge to follow my progress with binoculars.

Lassitude floods over me. I stop after every ten steps. I am moving desperately slow. I am ready to quit. The hours run on and I fear I won't have time enough to get back to my tent before dark. But I can't give up so close to the summit.

It is three o'clock when I reach the highest point of Kanchenjunga. Buffeted by gusts of wind, I shiver. Only Everest rises higher on the horizon. I am on the isolated spot that has haunted my dreams for eight months. Deep down, I feel a great joy but am too exhausted, too anxious

Pierre Beghin on Kanchenjunga. PHOTO: ANNIE BEGHIN/FOC PHOTO

about the descent, to have it come to the surface. A bluish haze of twilight floods the atmosphere. I must leave this icy summit. In less than three hours it will be inky black.

AN INTERVIEW WITH
DEREK HERSEY

by Annie Whitehouse

*D*uring the decade he spent in the United States, British climber Derek *Hersey stunned the American climbing community with countless ropeless ascents of difficult rock climbs ranging from small crag routes to what once were multiday aid lines up The Diamond, a 1,000-foot cliff on the 2,000-foot east face of Longs Peak (14,255) in Colorado's Rocky Mountain National Park. While so-called sport climbing flourished around him, with its emphasis on low-risk, technically arduous gymnastic movement, Hersey's roots in adventure climbing expressed themselves in his bold, spontaneous solos. The following interview—conducted by Annie Whitehouse, accomplished climber and personal friend of Hersey— echoes the sentiments of two other great free soloers of the modern era, American John Bachar and Canadian Peter Croft.*

Shortly after this interview, Hersey died while free soloing the Steck/Salathe route on Yosemite's Sentinel Rock. As the route was two letter-grades easier than what Hersey routinely soloed, climbers have speculated about all but one thing: free soloing can be a deadly business, even when performed by one of the best who has ever climbed.

‡   ‡   ‡

The rock in the enormous left-facing dihedral was wet and cold. Derek Hersey, clad in a single layer of baggy cotton clothing with his chalk bag tied loosely around his waist, was soloing on the lower left corner of The Diamond at 13,000-plus feet on Longs Peak. High above the Mills Glacier

Derek Hersey starting up the 1,000-foot vertical face of The Diamond on Longs Peak. Hersey climbed the face, downclimbed it, then climbed it again in one morning. PHOTO BY STEVE BARTLETT

and 450 feet up *Pervertical Sanctuary* (5.10), his third Grade IV solo of that July 1990 day, Hersey ground to a standstill. He was concerned that he might be off route, since the climbing seemed harder than 5.10. He yelled over to a friend, Steve Bartlett, on the nearby *Curving Vine,* for advice. Assured that he was on track, Hersey climbed out of sight.

"We didn't see him flying past," said Bartlett later, "so we figured he must have done it." From their stance on *Curving Vine,* Bartlett, an English climber who'd met Hersey ten years earlier, and his partner had watched Hersey psyching up to solo *Yellow Wall* (5.10) earlier that morning. "Derek sat at the base for about 20 minutes and then started," says Bartlett, a veteran soloist himself. "I could understand what he was going through."

By the time Bartlett and his partner had climbed three pitches, Hersey had completed the *Yellow Wall,* down soloed the *Casual Route* (5.10), and was well into *Pervertical Sanctuary.* Bartlett was astonished to see Hersey committed to *Pervertical Sanctuary,* knowing that he was climbing it onsight. "Watching Derek was like a breath of fresh air," Bartlett recalls, "so fast and efficient."

Hersey's on-sight solos of hard, multipitch routes on The Diamond and in Colorado's Black Canyon evoke a multitude of reactions from others. Mary Riedmiller, a longtime friend of Hersey's, recalls the rumors circulating around Eldorado Canyon after Hersey had soloed *The Naked Edge* (5.11b) in August 1984, five months after he had arrived in Boulder. "People didn't know who he was," says Riedmiller. "He was supposed to be a rich Englishman who had lost his fortune, was profoundly depressed and had come to Boulder to lose his life."

Many people admire his style. Others doubt his sanity, nicknaming him Doctor Death. In either case, his bold solos and wild appearance have fostered a mysterious reputation.

Hersey describes himself as "a simple man." He says that his life revolves around rock climbing, most often solo, almost every day. When off the rock, he finds pleasure in chess, music and socializing with his mates in Boulder. Hersey has few possessions or obligations, and has made climbing into a basic, uncomplicated way of life.

For Hersey, a typical climbing day starts slowly. He wakes up on the late side and drinks numerous cups of tea, English-style, laden with milk and sugar. Once alert, he starts a stream of consciousness flow of chatter with whomever is around. The talk continues throughout the day.

Usually he hitchhikes out to Eldorado Canyon around 10 A.M. He jokes with the rangers about punching in at the office. Armed for the day with only a chalk bag, shoes and a few candy bars, he hikes up to the day's first climb. Along the trail, he chats gregariously with tourists and climbers alike. By late afternoon, Hersey will have typically soloed 20 climbs, going from one end of the canyon to the other. His day ends with more bantering in the parking lot while he looks for a ride back to Boulder.

Often the climbs Hersey solos are Eldorado classics, long and sustained, such as the *Northwest Corner* (5.10c) of the Bastille. He combines those with shorter, more technically demanding climbs that are closer in grade to his on-sight leading ability, which is 5.12a—such as *Sidewall* (5.11c) and *Climb of the Century* (5.11b/c). Hersey made the second solo of *The Naked Edge* (5.lla), Eldorado's most heralded line, and has subsequently soloed it three more times. Recently he soloed *Jules Verne* (5.11b/c) and the *West Overhang* (5.11a) of the Maiden, two very exposed Front Range testpieces, on one hot summer afternoon.

Hersey's climbing style is smooth and intuitive. He moves precisely, with eloquent patience and calm. To compensate for a surprising lack of flexibility, he places his body in creative positions, often using smears and sideways stances. Watching him solo is like watching water flow.

Many Front Range routes bear Hersey's signature, including the unrepeated testpiece, *To R.P. or Not to Be* (5.12 VS [very serious]). Route names such as *She's a Soft Scrubber, Work Is the Scourge of the Climbing Class, The Yorkshire Ripper,* and *Mushy Peas* reveal both his understated British humor and a strong bond to his northern England heritage. Hersey guards his British persona fiercely. He still speaks with a pointedly strong Manchester accent and uses colloquialisms unique to his upbringing in the rough, industrial midlands. He will tell you, proudly, about what he eats and drinks: a typically English diet of meat and potatoes and loads of good ale. Hersey and his two British housemates, hungry for firsthand information from home, welcome a constant parade of touring British climbers into their house.

To return to England, Hersey admits, would be hard. He finds the economic possibilities, the drier climate, and the abundance of rock in the United States more conducive to his climbing lifestyle. While his mates in England turn to "the dole," the British equivalent of welfare, to provide time and money for climbing, Hersey supports himself with the occasional odd job, by guiding and by giving slide shows. Congenial yet enigmatic, he has found a unique niche for himself among today's fulltime climbers.

What brought you to the United States?

Five years unemployed in England solid. I came back from Verdon in October 1983 and I was in the cafe at Stoney Middleton and I thought, "I think I'll go over to America." Sold all me ice gear to get to New York. When I left England people said I would only last here two weeks. I've been here eight years making people suffer.

There seems to be a big difference between the economic background of American and British climbers.

In Britain, especially when I started climbing, all the climbers usually came from the city. Nine times out of ten you come from a working-class background. In America, the standard of living's higher. Usually, the person in the street is not going to pick up climbing.

So, how did you pick up climbing?

Me father's a proper hiker, so he'd go hiking every week. He introduced me to the outdoors, which from Manchester's only 20 miles away. I had Derbyshire, the Peak District National Park, right on me doorstep. Lots of gritstone, God's own rock, you know.

How about your mom, did she hike?

No, me mum doesn't quite really understand it. She thinks climbing is going hiking up rocks. Me mum's out to lunch.

You've been climbing for 17 years. Who were some of your role models when you started?

Don Whillans and Joe Brown were the yardstick, and you aspired to their routes. And later on Pete Livesey, who set a new standard of climbing. He brought in training; nobody could understand why he was so fit. Ron Fawcett was me other hero; he was totally out there. And Dougie Hall, who's only 5' 4," he's like the male version of Lynn Hill. He went through three or four belayers in a day because people just couldn't keep up with him.

Didn't you repeat a bold Livesey route, Footless Crow, *in 1982?*

All Livesey's routes had been repeated apart from this one. The Lake District lads, they couldn't touch it. They were getting dead frustrated and it was like the major route to go for. Then Jerry Moffat and Dougie Hall repeated it, but I don't think anyone expected me to come along. If you fell off the crux, you could hit a slab 40 feet down. On undercut, loose flakes there was a long reach left and just one #5 RP for gear. Plus the route had a reputation. A repeat can be harder than a first ascent, in kind of a strange way, because of the reputation. Psychologically it was a major breakthrough for me.

It was an on-sight flash for you, but didn't Livesey preview and rehearse some of his routes? That's contrary to the ground-up, on-sight ethic usually associated with British rock climbing of that time.

Yeah, he previewed it. In the 1970s they'd go out in midweek when no one was looking and do the odd shady business: rappel down, preinspect and clean the climb. The idea being if you're going to clean it, you might as well have a look at the moves. It was happening but it wasn't exposed, as it were. I wish I had me microphone then.

What did you think of Livesey's style?

I wasn't quite sure where to place him at first. But looking at his routes and having done most of his major testpieces of the late 1970s and early 1980s, I respect the guy even more now.

It sounds like lots of talented climbers come from your area.

There was Jerry Moffat, Steve Bancroft, bundles of talent coming out, mostly from Manchester and Sheffield. Again, it was the working-class northern English cities that were producing the best goods. When we came out from the factories I think we sharpened our skills, just like Don (Whillans) and Joe (Brown).

You and Moffat have gone in different directions. Moffat is more of a sport climber nowadays and you're not. Was sport climbing an option when you climbed in England?

There was no concept of sport climbing. It seemed very clear; you went climbing on grit, and then you climbed in the Peak District, and then you went to Wales and the Lakes and Scotland, and then you went to the Alps. It was a very traditional progression.

What do you think of sport climbing, using a toprope to rehearse hard moves on well-protected climbs, with a redpoint ascent as the goal?

The 1990s word is "working." Work the route, work the moves. I think to enjoy climbing is to be nearly at your limit, but not over it. That's why I don't hangdog and stuff—it's over the limit and out of context. The other reason is probably stronger. I won't hangdog because I solo quite often, and with soloing, hangdogging is a bad habit to get into. Also, I'm kind of lazy. It's just too much work. Mention work and I run away.

Don't you find any satisfaction in working on a hard climb and getting it?

The least satisfaction, because it's 7-11 climbing. And if it's convenient, it's nice. No risk. Ten quickdraws, you don't have to hang around placing wires. But I'll never climb 5.13 because I like soloing so much.

What's your margin of safety when you on-sight solo a hard climb like Country Club Crack *(5.11b/c)?*

It's probably better than when I'm climbing with a rope. You have to almost say there is no probability of falling. Subconsciously you just have to go with that.

You are soloing climbs that are only a few letter grades below your on-sight leading ability. You can only gloss over the risk so much—in reality, any false move creates a high probability of death.

If it does, it does. I don't view it that way. Climbing's supposed to be simple. When you're up there soloing, you're just presented with what's presented. One on one, it's very simple math. You can't start throwing algebra into it: w over k equals y plus z.

What happens when you find yourself in a dicey spot?

I keep me drive going—I just carry on through with it. I deal with what I've got right there. No time for foo-fooing around. Part of the soloing game is not to throw both dice. You either come down or go through all the way. If you stop halfway, you'll end up in the box.

How do you choose your solos?

Like anything else, the drive has to be right, especially with soloing. Like when I soloed *Death and Transfiguration* (5.11b). It's one of the best 5.11s on the Front Range. It was like, how can I not solo this? It was just great. Seventy feet of pure great moves!

You had climbed Death and Transfiguration *once before with a rope. Do you tend to favor soloing routes you've already done?*

If you're soloing something because you've already led it, you're trying to put a square in a circle. You might as well be on two different climbs—they're two very different feelings. Sometimes it's a disadvantage to have climbed the route before. You can come across a spot that you passed easily with a rope, but it can become the crux when soloing. Don't even play that game, it'll spit you out.

You soloed three routes in one day on The Diamond in July 1990. Tell us about that.

After the first 50 feet of the *Yellow Wall* (5.10), I started getting into gear. I started into a flow and didn't stop. I didn't stop at the belay ledges, but motored on by. There was a wet section on the fourth pitch. It was the only section I stopped at, for ten or 12 minutes. It was soaking wet, both me hands were soaking wet. I'd free climbed the *Yellow Wall* five or six years ago and that section wasn't wet then. I went up the *Forrest Finish* (5.10) to Table Ledge as well, which I'd never done before—three pitches of beautiful 5.10 cracks.

That part took you 20 minutes, then you downclimbed the Casual Route (5.10). *Had you been on the* Casual Route *before?*

Once, yeah. Years ago, but coming down stuff's always different. I got down the *Casual Route* and then I saw *Pervertical Sanctuary.* I was, well, wired. I mean, nothing's gonna stop me now.

Then you soloed Pervertical Sanctuary *on-sight. How did you feel after all that?*

Derek Hersey (right-center of photo) takes a solo Scenic Cruise *in the 2,000-foot-high Black Canyon of the Gunnison, Colorado.* PHOTO BY DAN HARE

I felt great! I was on cloud nine, you know. I was still high, like, four hours later. I had a couple of bottles of Sheaf Stout waiting for me in the boulder field. Just sitting in the sun, drinking Sheaf by 11 A.M. Very relaxed and very happy. The meeting of mind and body is very satisfying. High adrenaline. Very simple.

A year later you soloed three big routes—Scenic Cruise (5.10), Journey Home (5.10) and Leisure Climb (5.9)—in the Black Canyon of the Gunnison.

The Black Canyon's a very deep, atmospheric place to be without a rope. You're bound to have a little bit of apprehension when you embark on something there. Soloing in places like that is like rising to the occasion.

You did something like 35 pitches. What do you recall most about that day?

Getting up the first 300 or 400 feet was like me warm-up. I felt like I was just getting to know the Black Canyon. I remember looking across and measuring how high I was getting by the other wall. The sixth pitch of the *Scenic Cruise* is pegmatite, an exposed 5.10 traverse. That's when you know you've left the secure crack systems and you're really in the Black Canyon.

Have you been criticized for soloing?

A lot of people want to know, "What's making you tick?" The reason people don't like soloing at a high level is because the total mental aspect is too much. Most of the time, you get compliments and then they go, "That's crazy," which is like saying one thing and doing another. Soloing is kind of a selfish way of climbing but I enjoy meself. One of the reasons I want to solo is because I want to do it by meself. Not to be antisocial, but I love just climbing by meself. I know my talents and skills. I've got a very good temperament and you have to have a little bit of ego to go with it, for sure. Soloing's definitely kind of an ego thing.

What about people who are climbing consistently at a 5.13 level but would not dare solo at 5.10? Do you have a problem with that?

No. I think it's kind of apples and oranges. Dale Goddard or Jim Karn go off and do a 5.14—and good for them. Each to their own, as they say. If you had a big ego problem and did a lot of soloing like I do, you'd be out there saying, "Dale, go solo *The Naked Edge.*" I would never suggest to anyone on a serious note that they go out and solo. I might say go lead something, but that's different. You get gear in. We used to do that all the time in England. Go and sandbag people.

Not only in England, but here too! What about your unrepeated route in Eldorado, To R.P. or Not to Be *(5.12 VS)?*

Yeah, that's still waiting for some punters to come along. I was telling Patrick Edlinger and Wolfgang Gullich, "Have I got the route for you!" but they wanted to do *Desdichado* instead. When I put that route up I'd just come back from Verdon. I'd been clipping bolts for two months. I knew it was a great line to go up that wall. And there's no way off it once you start. It is nice to have a route that is unrepeated, but it would be great to see someone do it.

What do you aspire to in roped climbing?

The on-sight flash. There's nothing more perfect. If I'm climbing at 5.10, 5.11, 5.12 and I on-sight flash the route, then that's as good as it gets. You only get one chance for the on-sight flash.

Many climbers say that the fastest way to develop strength and improve performance is to work the moves on climbs much harder than they can lead on-sight. How do you train for strength and endurance?

There was a time in England we went to the gym. It was an interesting test. And then straight after that we'd go and drink eight pints of beer and eat about six cheese-and-onion sandwiches. Turned out it helped our finger strength. I must have built me stamina up there.

You don't train now, but the type of climbing you do requires all kinds of strength and stamina. How do you explain that?

I'm always climbing. It wouldn't matter now if I did 200 pull-ups or whatever. It wouldn't mean a damn in me climbing. It's two things now: I've been climbing a long time, and I've put so much work into it at me own steady pace. And I'm definitely mentally as strong now as ever.

In heaven: Hersey relaxes with his other passion after a day of soloing. PHOTO BY DAN HARE

Any tips for climbers who want to improve their on-sight leading ability?

If you climb 5.9, the best thing to do is to go out and climb lots of 5.7, 5.8, and 5.9 pitches. All the time, different routes, bundles of routes. Not at your limit, just underneath. And lead them as much as possible. That'll do it. Climbing's still very simple and very basic. It's physical and it's mental. Obviously, you've got to have the right tools for the trade, but I think it's more important to go with an attitude of, "You're as good as you are."

SOLO ON THE CHARMOZ

by Mark Twight

*M*ark Twight carved himself a distinctive niche in the American
climbing scene by fashioning his career on the European model.
Specializing in neither rock climbing nor high mountaineering, but
rather in "alpine" climbing, Twight focused much of his abundant energy on
the Alps in Europe; his accomplishments have reflected a bold streak bordering,
at times, on the seemingly insane. His steady stream of articles are bursting with
angst, poetry, self-absorption, ingenuity, brooding, ecstasy and all the other
passions that drive a solo alpine climber onto mountains of rock and ice.

‡   ‡   ‡

In your letter you asked where I've been; oh, the usual Chamonix hangs
I suppose. The waiting is so frustrating and they don't even seem to notice. Things are not the same any longer, something has changed. Before,
I thought that I was going to stay the winter and I do not know quite what
happened to change my mind. Something was stretched too tightly and
it snapped, I began to hear a little voice—a voice that I'd turned away
from earlier. I had managed to ignore it for a long time, but now it was
utterly screaming, *"Get out Mark, it is time to go home!"*

So what now? What happened? You'll ask. Things were tough but
going pretty well. It was my birthday so I decided to treat myself to the
north face of the Grandes Charmoz. My friends had all gone home in
October so I'd be soloing again, but I felt comfortable with the process.

The Charmoz is a difficult climb—what we did on the Eiger was of-
fensively easy by comparison—and I was caught in a storm near the top,

a storm that wasn't supposed to arrive for another twelve hours. Hard luck I guess, and it scared me quite badly, what with the Welzenbach horror stories and all. So I began to rush things a bit, became a little careless perhaps. I expected the Heckmair finish to be a cruise because the crux is purportedly in the rock bands down low. But I was wrong; the ice was extremely thin over very steep rock, and it was rotten, hollow ice in places, which made things worse.

The ice that my feet had been gently resting on parted from the rock and my frontpoints scraped down the featureless ice beneath. I smoothly transferred my weight to my tools, only to see one rip out of the rot it had been placed in. Once again I had but one point of contact with the ice, with the world. One inch of tempered steel between me and Icarus. I thrashed around, seeking the holds that would save my life. Sparks showered down as I struck at patches of stuff that weren't even ice and the pick bounced uselessly off the rock. My head spun with fear—I had the sensation of falling over backwards, and tumbling, tumbling end over end. My head broke open like a carelessly dropped cantaloupe and my precious life made an ugly mess of the icefield below me. No witnesses, no shock, just a lonely ending, a soloist's end.

The music on my Walkman shouted:

"I was going to drown, but then I started swimming.
I was going down but then I started winning."

I did find holds. I did get my feet stemmed out onto good ice and I pulled up. I pulled for all I was worth, I made it fit back together. Moments later I found myself at a relatively secure rest. It was snowing harder by then.

I was shaking, barely holding it together, but holding it because I had to, because I needed to keep climbing because the hardest part—finding a way down—still loomed ahead of me. I turned up the volume.

I crested the ridge in a whiteout and didn't bother with the summit, which was 200 feet away. I jumped into the nearest couloir I saw, figuring that as long as it didn't cliff out I'd be able to get down.

Descent, Descend . . . Sanctuary, Survival: there were primary functions only, no hunger, no thirst, no philosophizing—only a high standard of action. I was really frightened by this point. "Why does luck run out all at once? And never by degrees . . ."

I downclimbed until it became too steep and then began rappelling, leaving gear behind without caring because money made absolutely no sense at the time. I was forced to rappel off single anchors as I had so few, and that was playing for all the marbles at every throw. Then the avalanches began; small ones at first, but growing larger and larger as more snow fell and I put more above me by losing altitude. Often without warning a slide would roar down. I'd just sink my ice tools and hope that it wasn't too big and that there were no rocks in it. I descended faster than ever before: overcoming my best efforts as I was pushed closer to the edge.

Eventually I reached relatively level ground, sanctuary that caused me to breathe a little more easily. Still I did not know where I stood, nor was there any way of finding out. I had dealt with the worst part and I believed that I could handle the rest of the journey. I used my instincts and got myself out—being lost seemed trivial compared to what I just came through.

But there was nothing for me in the valley: no comfort, no understanding, no friends to return to. I was still alone at a time when that was the last thing I wanted. I had chosen to be alone in the first place, that was a month ago though, before the *Super Couloir*, before the Charmoz, not today. I don't want to stand alone, I don't want to stay here any longer. The voice is saying "Go home," and I cannot argue with it now, I do not have the energy. I am coming home.

A warm smile, a last hand to shake and fond "adieu," but never "Good-bye."

"From my head to my toes, through my teeth, through my nose, you get these words wrong . . . you get these words wrong. From my head to my toes, from my knees to my eyes, every time I watch the skies—but for these last few days leave me alone. For these last few days leave me alone . . . just leave me alone."

DENALI WINTER SOLOS: ALONE IN ONE OF THE HARSHEST ENVIRONMENTS ON EARTH

by Art Davidson

*M*ountains are often measured in superlatives, and Denali (Mount McKinley, 20,320 feet) tops the list in two categories: in terms of vertical rise from base to summit, Denali is the biggest mountain on earth; and evidenced by actual records and testimonies of mountaineers, no peak combines such extremes of cold, altitude, high winds and darkness. Despite these hazards, every year Denali draws hundreds of mountaineers to its flanks. About half experience the joy of summiting. Others are turned back by the raging winds, plunging temperatures, hidden crevasses, and whiteout conditions. Every few years, a handful of climbers approach Denali during the most grievous time of year — winter. Then there are those precious few who take this dire venture one step further . . . and go it alone. As you will hear in the next narrative, the first solo winter ascent of Denali was a high stakes game of roulette that demanded inordinate willpower, skill, strength and judgement.

   In 1967, author Art Davidson made the first winter ascent of Denali with a team of climbers — an extreme experience captured in Davidson's much praised book Minus 148 Degrees. On the expedition, one team member died and several were frostbitten. Three reached the summit only to be trapped by winds in excess of 100 miles per hour. As the storm raged on, day after day, their companions gave them up for dead and began descending. But the three held on in a makeshift snow cave. They made it through by their sheer will to survive — and by sticking together. Davidson, an Alaska resident and accomplished climber who enjoys soloing on *occasion, is uniquely qualified to present us with the story of four climbers who stood on the shoulders of his team's accomplishments and raised the bar even further—by attempting to solo Denali in winter, quite possibly the harshest environment on earth.*

‡ ‡ ‡

The high, cold ridges of Denali have a way of calling to mountaineers, including the solo climbers who live on the edge, forever redrawing the line between what's possible and impossible. At 20,320 feet, Denali rises further from its base to its summit than any other mountain in the world, making it the biggest mountain on earth. It tests climbers, even the most skilled, with its cold, thin air, hidden crevasses and sudden storms. For some, a solo climb of Denali is a surreal dance with the elements which at some point turns into an all or nothing affair: you either make the spectacular climb, or you die. For others, a solo climb of Denali is a process of carefully calculating the risks and preserving a margin of safety, however thin, so they can return to the mountains another day.

I first went to Denali with my friend Shiro Nishimae and the Osaka Alpine Club. While we watched huge cornices soften and crumble in the July sun, we tried to imagine the winter storms that packed snow into these massive formations. What would the temperature drop to in February? What would the wind be like? And we shuddered to think of Denali's most eerie winter aspect—the darkness. The high ridges would block out the low winter sun, allowing the basins to receive only a few hours of twilight between long nights. Could a person survive up there in winter, let alone climb?

By January of 1967, I was off with Shiro and six other friends to try to make the first winter ascent of Denali. The higher we climbed the more we felt we'd entered some other world, utterly cold and desolate but with a haunting beauty all its own. One evening, Shiro, Dave Johnston and I were climbing up to 17,000 feet in deep twilight that turned briefly to darkness before a full moon rose. The highest ridges of Foraker were already illumined with silver light. We paused to watch a sight never before seen— the full moon appearing from behind Denali's southern flank, lighting, each in its turn, the sweeping ice and rock couloirs of the range.

To the north there rolled away an expanse of low, silver clouds, broken only by two hills rising into the moonlight like a pair of white whales surfacing. To the south, a sea of clouds rolled away unbroken to the horizon. Resting at the col, our eyes traveled over endless variations of ice not apparent in daylight. The long, snow-covered ridges of the Denali massif flowed into the sea of clouds like white rivers into estuaries of darkness.

We managed to complete our winter climb that year, but not unscathed. Jacques Batkin, perhaps our physically strongest climber, died in a crevasse fall. Then after reaching the summit in the dark, the temperature 57 below, Dave Johnston, Ray Genet and I descended into our own moment of truth—a moment that would last six days as hurricane-force winds lashed Denali's upper slopes.

We were bivouacking at Denali Pass when the storm hit. It felt as if gravity had shifted, had become some horizontal force that threatened to send us flying across the slope. The combination of wind and air temperature resulted in a wind-chill somewhere off the chart, minus 148 degrees. We scooped out a shallow cave and retreated under the ice. After three days, our companions at a lower camp gave us up for dead, certain that there was no way we could still be alive. But we hung on. After six days, the wind finally quieted and the three of us staggered down with frostbitten hands and feet.

After our return it was, of course, only a matter of time before someone would try a solo winter ascent of Denali. Going alone would be logistically more difficult, of course, and with almost no margin for error, the level of risk would be ratcheted up several notches. I remember thinking that whoever set himself to this forlorn mission would be drawn by powerful, perhaps complex, inner yearnings.

The first to try Denali alone in winter was Jonathan Waterman, a superb technical climber with an obsessive, and perhaps ultimately psychotic, inner drive. He had led a hard route on El Capitan, a 3,000-foot rock face in Yosemite Valley. And he'd led the crux pitches of Huntington's East Ridge that David Roberts describes in his book *The Mountain of My Fear* as a horror of "huge hanging glaciers, the most dangerous formations imaginable, sprawled obscenely down the ridge."

Later, Waterman would spend 145 days alone on nearby Mount Hunter. He had trained for this climb by submerging himself in tubs of ice, but nothing could fully prepare his psyche for being alone in such an exposed and inhospitable place for nearly five months. Forty-three days into his Mount Hunter expedition, both Waterman's food and morale were running low. He was struck with periods of extreme loneliness. There were times he broke down crying with frustration. An airdrop from bush pilot Cliff Hudson refurbished his supplies, but his relation to the mountain had taken an unusual turn. As he confided to a friend: something "far more precious would be lost if I lived through (this climb of Hunter) than if I died. Living through it would mean that Nature wasn't as raw as everyone wanted to believe it was. Living through it would mean that Mount Hunter wasn't the mountain that I thought it was."

Despite this Faustian ambivalence toward his own life, Waterman fixed 3,600 feet of rope down the north ridge for his descent. He then climbed to the summit, surviving two falls that he acknowledged, "Could have been fatal."

By any measure, Waterman's solo climb of Hunter's south ridge was an extraordinary accomplishment; some have ranked it up there with the first ascents of Yosemite's huge walls and other incredible climbing achievements. But Waterman got scant recognition. He returned to Talkeetna so broke that he had to borrow $20 from pilot Hudson and accept the only job available. "After this horrible climb—or, actually, this superb climb," he said, "my only societal reward was to be washing dishes at the very bottom of society."

An acquaintance, Lance Leslie, said that Waterman seemed a changed person after the climb: "Waterman was odd, but little different than other climbers with his scruffy beard and down feathers clinging to his matted hair. But after Hunter he seemed almost dangerously psychotic."

In December of 1979, Waterman made his first trip to Denali in winter. Hudson dropped him off on the Kahiltna with 500 pounds of food. He'd come to climb the hideously steep, avalanche-raked south face. He had a personal connection to this route: a close friend, who later died on K2, had made the first direct ascent of this wall in summer. Waterman hoped that climbing such a severe route by himself in winter would earn him a permit for a solo winter ascent of Mount Everest. He also confided to a friend that his quest was, at least in part, to win his father's approval.

Nevertheless, after ten days of staring up at the imposing rock and hanging glaciers of the south face, he called Hudson and requested that the pilot come pick him up: "Take me home," he said. "I don't want to die." Safely back in Talkeetna, he said "the mountain defeated me, but it didn't eat me alive."

For Waterman, Denali seemed to be transforming into an animate being—not clearly a friend nor fully an adversary, but some sentient presence with whom he had his own personal relationship. "More than his fellow humans, the mountains had become his companions," wrote Ingrid Canfield in the book *Skiing Down Everest and Other Crazy Adventures.* "And he invested them with the frailties and duplicities, the enticements and charms of real people, relating to their power and responding to them only with his true essence."

Two months after coming off Denali's south face, Waterman's cabin near Talkeetna burned to the ground. Gone were not just clothes and climbing gear, but years of meticulous notes from his solitary sojourns. Waterman told those watching the smoldering ruins that these notes were the essence of himself, that losing them this way meant he, too, had burned up in the fire.

Waterman checked himself into the Alaska Psychiatric Hospital. Two weeks later, he abruptly checked himself out—and began laying plans for his return to Denali in winter. But two years would pass—two years of living a marginal existence in Fairbanks, where he became something of a local cult hero, regaling others with tales of his months spent alone on airy ledges of ice and rock. Still, his relationship with the mountain remained conflicted, unresolved.

Waterman's final reconciliation began in February 1981. He started hiking from the shores of Cook Inlet some 60 miles south of Talkeetna. Ten days later he staggered into the Talkeetna Motel. It was past midnight and he was soaked from falling through river ice. After drying his clothes and getting a couple good meals under his belt, he continued on, struggling over frozen muskeg, 35 miles up the Chulitna, Tokositna and Ruth Rivers to the 2,000-foot level on Denali. But something wasn't quite right. He said his stove was malfunctioning, and returned to Talkeetna. Here he must have wrestled again with his inner demons, steeling himself for the long-awaited resolution.

Then one day, Waterman returned the citizen-band radio he'd borrowed from Cliff Hudson and told his pilot friend, "I won't be seeing you again." Hudson flew him to the mountain, where Waterman milled about at 6,000 feet on the Ruth glacier for a few weeks. On the first of April, he headed up, without a sleeping bag. Before him lay a route so riddled with crevasses that even the renowned Reinhold Messner, first to solo Mount Everest, had deemed it too dangerous.

Later, some climbers found a box of food on which Waterman had written "the last kiss." He was never seen again.

On the first day of February three years later, Naomi Uemura strapped on his snowshoes, pulled on an enormous pack and, as he had so many times before, set out to accomplish something that had never been done. His goal was the dream, or vexation, that had taken John Waterman's life—a solo winter ascent of Denali.

Uemura was as ready for this task as any man alive. He wasn't a gifted technical climber like Waterman, but he knew the mountain and he knew how to survive in extreme conditions. In July, 14 years earlier, he had made the first solo summer ascent of Denali, reaching the summit by the same West Buttress route that now lay before him in February.

Born in southwest Japan in 1941, Uemura was a university student when he discovered mountains. He was drawn not to steep technical climbs but to wandering alone among the peaks, finding peace and solitude. At the age of 25, he went to Europe, climbing alone in the Alps and narrowly escaping disaster in a crevasse fall on Mont Blanc. Over the next five years, he wandered from continent to continent, developing the skills and the reputation of an adventurer. Once, after climbing Aconcagua, the highest peak in South America, he built a raft and floated the full length of the Amazon. In 1969, Uemura became the first Japanese to reach the summit of Mount Everest. Such was the spirit of this incredible man.

After Everest, Uemura was drawn to the North and South Poles. One of his first trips was an incredible 7,500 mile, three-year dogsled journey from Greenland, across northern Canada to Alaska. Then, in 1978, he set out from Ellesmere Island with 17 dogs for a solo trek to the North Pole. It was winter with only a few hours of daylight and the temperature hovering around fifty below. A few days into his trek, he was attacked by a polar bear that chased away his dogs, tore open his tent, pawed at his sleeping bag while he was in it and then unaccountably went away. Uemura tracked down his dogs and continued north, cutting a path through ridges of windblown snow and jumbled blocks of ice that had thwarted larger expeditions.

Naomi Uemura made it to the North Pole.

So it was that Uemura came to Denali in the winter of 1984 uniquely experienced and toughened for this solo ascent. Unlike Waterman, whose climbing achievements were all but unknown, Uemura enjoyed a reputation as one of the world's most accomplished explorers and adventurers. In Japan he was a legend, to some an immortal, indomitable spirit. While Waterman had scraped at the margins of society for a meager existence, Uemura had people eager to sponsor his adventures. He was a mainstream hero.

Before flying to Denali from Talkeetna, Uemura appeared calm and self-assured. There seemed little doubt that he would succeed. Only later would friends recall that he was in a hurry. He had a solo dog-mushing trek across Antarctica coming up. Hearing that others, including Dave Johnston (who had been on the first winter ascent with me in 1967), were thinking of trying Denali alone in winter, Uemura wanted to squeeze in yet another historic achievement. He planned to climb Denali fast—in one week, only a fraction of the time most climbers allow for acclimatization and bad weather.

Uemura flew to the Kahiltna and started up with a 40-pound pack of caribou meat, seal oil, and three liters of fuel. The weather was cold, but clear and stable. With no one to hold him back, he climbed quickly. On February 12, his 43rd birthday, he was spotted above 18,000 feet. He radioed pilot Lowell Thomas Jr. that he expected to reach the summit by 4 P.M.

The next day Thomas flew by the mountain again. Uemura radioed that he'd reached the summit about 7 P.M. the previous night. He had descended for about three hours, was cold, but okay. He asked to be picked up in two days, on February 15, at his Base Camp on the Kahiltna.

On February 15, pilot Doug Geeting flew to the Kahiltna Base Camp. Uemura was not there, nor was there any sign he'd been there since the start of the climb. Geeting, joined by Thomas, flew the upper reaches of the mountain. The sky was still clear, but a lenticular cloud cap was forming over the summit. There was no sign of Uemura. The pilots figured he was probably holed up in a snow cave, waiting for the wind to die down.

Confusing messages began coming back from the mountain. One pilot thought he saw Uemura waving from a snow cave at about 16,000 feet. Another thought he heard a short radio transmission—"I'm lost." For the next three days a storm with high winds closed in around Denali. When the weather broke on February 20, Geeting and Thomas were up flying at daybreak. They knew that if Uemura was alive, he should be descending. For more than five hours, the pilots searched the West Buttress route. They saw no one. They saw no tracks.

Naomi Uemura had vanished.

By the time Uemura was reported missing, Dave Johnston had already packed food for his own, long-planned solo winter ascent. As concern mounted for the missing climber, Dave wrote in his journal: "Naomi loved Denali. He gambled and sadly lost. It's unthinkable—one of the world's experts on high altitude and cold weather has disappeared. Some of my friends, saddened by Naomi's death, are worrying excessively about me. I explain that my style will be totally different: 90 days of food and fuel, backed by 1,000 feet of fixed rope. But my friends are upset. I hate bending people out of shape with worry. The timing is just off."

Dave canceled his 1984 plans to solo Denali in winter. But he would return—in mid-February, two years later in 1986, 19 years after Dave, Ray Genet and I had made the first winter ascent.

Always an admirer of the early "Sourdough" climbers who had headed out for Denali on foot from Fairbanks, Dave eschewed a quick flight to Base Camp at 7,500 feet on the Kahiltna. Shouldering his pack and strapping on a hauling sled, he headed out from his cabin, 60 miles from the mountain. It was perfect winter weather: a stable high pressure area kept the sky cloudless and the temperature between zero and twenty above.

Wanting to make the climb quietly, he had let only a handful of people know he was heading up. But by the time he reached Kahiltna Pass, news reporters had found him out and were falling all over themselves to follow his progress.

The good weather held and Dave quickly ferried a supply of food and fuel to his high camps. At 6' 6" with sinewy, giraffe-like legs and powerful lungs, Dave could move as fast as anyone at high altitude. But he wasn't trying to blitz his way up and down the mountain like Uemura had. Nor was he throwing his fate to the elements, as Waterman had. Dave was climbing cautiously, having the time of his life—trucking along, a big grin on his face, taking his giant strides and singing to himself.

By March 1, he had hauled supplies up to the 13,500-foot level, almost within striking distance of the summit. He rested, gathered himself, and watched the weather closely. When the moment felt right, he would set out for the top with his sleeping bag, a week's worth of food and his snow shovel. If the weather held he could reach the top and be back in a day or two. If a storm clamped down on the mountain, he'd simply dig a snow cave and burrow in. Dave was in his element.

Then the wind came up. Dave dug into the slope. After huddling in his cave for several hours he heard strange noises outside. "It went pitter-patter, just like footsteps on the snow. This was no hallucination. I heard it for sure."

Dave dismissed the idea that he was hearing the kind of ghostly apparition some climbers on Everest and other high peaks have reported—appearances of mystery climbers or mountaineers known to have died there. Perhaps the wind was blowing his gear around. He had to see what was going on.

Trying to look outside, Dave discovered that snow had packed shut the entrance of his cave, a potentially fatal situation. Both shovels were outside, so he began digging his way through with a cooking pot. He dug through four feet of snow but the entrance was still sealed shut. Dave was being entombed in the mountain by the wind and driving snow; he couldn't help wondering, had this been Uemura's fate?

"I was getting a little antsy," Dave said, "so I broke a hole through the roof and popped outside. I was really getting hammered—the wind was blowing 60, 70 miles an hour."

In the fury of the storm, Dave set about rebuilding the cave, patching the roof, digging a new entrance. Those curious sounds that he had heard, apparition or not, had succeeded in driving him from the comfort of his sleeping bag to dig his way out of his buried cave. The sounds had, in effect, saved his life. He got his sheltered repaired, but his feet suffered. "I went back in and brewed up some tea. Two toes were white. I rubbed them. Then came that old familiar feeling—like a dog nipping at your toes."

Dave had frostbite. "It's so ironic," he told me later, "it was the old frostbite injury from our winter climb in '67. It never completely recovered. In the best of times, some of my toes are a little numb and I guess that's why I didn't feel them getting cold."

Strangely, it had been on March 1, 1967—exactly 19 years earlier to the day—that Dave had first frozen his feet while digging the snow cave that saved our lives. Now, alone and high on Denali, his freezing feet left Dave no choice but to abandon his quest. When the wind slacked off, he skied back down the Kahiltna, and across 60 miles of frozen wilderness to his cabin at Trapper Creek.

"I know I could've made the summit," he said later. "It's disappointing. I got all the hard work done—all the 150-pound relays—only to get stopped by a little thing like my toe."

Altogether, Dave had skied and climbed by himself for 150 miles. "It's so beautiful up there," he said. "The trip was worth it just to be on the mountain again."

After three solo attempts to climb Denali in winter, two men had died and the third came home with frostbite. While the summit had been reached by Uemura, no one had made it up and back alive—in other words, nobody had successfully climbed Denali solo in winter. The perils of the undertaking were becoming more obvious . . . and more inviting to those who look for extreme challenges.

Enter Vern Tejas. At 35, his lean body was toughened from years of climbing and leading rescues in the Alaska Range. His black beard was thick and tangled. Except for a thin ponytail falling to his broad shoulders, his head was shaved so smooth it glistened. Vern could look imposing, but his eyes usually betrayed a hint of mischief.

"So Vern," I asked him, "why are you going to take on this kind of risk?"

"Art, you know climbing doesn't make sense," he said. "It doesn't prove anything."

"Yeah, okay. But tell me, what's got you going up there alone in winter?"

"Well, it probably all started with the Buffalo Bayou," he said, that mischief shining in his eyes. "You see, I grew up on the outskirts of Houston, Texas. And as a little kid I used to disappear into the bayou. There were so many things to watch—hawks and hummingbirds, coyotes. And it was always peaceful. I learned how to catch snakes. Sometimes I'd camp out, listening to the night sounds and dreaming of being a Colorado mountain man."

When he was 15, his parents separated and Vern took off for the part of Colorado he'd heard was the wildest, most rugged place in the states. He started hitchhiking with some of his mother's pots and pans strapped to his back. He was armed with a quiver full of arrows and a bow as tall he was. When he saw a sign saying San Juan Mountains, he lit out across country. "I was looking for a wild place," he says. "I was going to go there and live off the land. But, boy, was it hard to catch something to eat. After a couple of weeks, I was so hungry I headed home."

Tejas returned to Texas and graduated from high school, but a wanderlust had been kindled. At 18 he had a falling out with his father. "It came to blows. I left and didn't talk to him again." Tejas went on the road, hitching rides and finding work where he could. In upstate New York he met a man who rock climbed, whose son had died in a plane crash in Alaska. Vern remembers that, "In me he found someone to share his love of heights. I wasn't a natural. I had to work hard at it. But I learned about ropes and rock."

Vern was also learning about himself. As a way of asserting his new identity, as well as making a symbolic break from his father, he changed his surname from Hansel to Tejas, which is pronounced Tay-hoss (the Spanish way of saying Texas) and means friendly in the dialect of the Caddo Indians.

With a new sense of himself, Tejas traveled through Canada. Near Whitehorse in the Yukon Territory, a man gave him a lift to Alaska. Along the way they stopped to watch clouds lift over Denali's Wickersham Wall: "It was like the mountain was forming right before our eyes. I've never seen anything so big. I knew right then I had to climb this mountain."

After working construction for five years, Vern had saved up enough money to pay for a guided trip on Denali. Not everyone in his group made the summit. Vern did. "I had to make it," said Vern, "'cause I was so broke I'd never be able to get back and try it again."

Tejas would return to Denali, again and again, first as a climbing assistant, then as a lead guide. The glaciers and high ridges became his workplace, his backyard, and a large part of his identity. "I love being in the mountains, " he says. "From them I get feelings of self-sufficiency, confidence and self-worth. And I like to help others find these things."

By the time I met Vern, his wanderlust had blossomed into a marvelous sense of adventure and communion with wild places. He struck me as one of those whose dreams, in the words of Antonio Machado, "have winding roads, labyrinthine paths . . . through darkness and silence; deep vaults, ladders over the stars."

Over the years he spent in high places, Vern began sensing a new dimension to his relationship with Denali—that deep vault of winter. "I knew my capabilities and margins of safety on the mountain, but only in summer," he said. "I wondered: what would they be in winter?"

Vern began planning his solo ascent two years in advance. Part of his strategy was to begin his climb not in winter, but in summer— and not in Alaska, but thousands of miles away in Argentina. There, in the southern hemisphere's summer, he acclimatized his body on the highest mountain in South America, 23,000-foot-high Aconcagua. After guiding an expedition, he climbed back up to the summit, dragging his mountain bike along—and then raced down. Then he reascended the peak with a parasail and literally flew off the mountain, gliding over the Andes for a full 20 minutes. With his conditioning complete, he hurried to Denali.

Upon landing in Anchorage from Buenos Aires, Tejas grabbed his previously packed supplies and flew to the Kahiltna. To survive something that had taken the lives of two of the three men who had gone before would take raw nerve and a sense of reality. Tejas had confidence in his ability, but he could also contemplate defeat. Before his climb he said, "I decided early on that I'd be willing to turn back, even if it meant that I was ridiculed by others. I know that going up there in winter is risky. But I know my limits. The summit could be right there in front of me, but if the risk is too great, I'll retreat. Reaching the summit is important, but it isn't everything."

Vern thought that anyone climbing solo without taking some sort of precautions was crazy. To arm himself against crevasses thinly-covered with wind-blown snow, he strapped on a 15-foot aluminum ladder as soon as he got on the glacier. If he fell into a hidden crevasse, the ladder would hopefully span the opening and hold him over the abyss. As an additional precaution, Tejas carried a rope to belay himself across the trickiest passages.

Unlike the unfettered Uemura, Vern was laden down with rope, ladder and extra food that slowed his progress up the mountain. His climbing was further hampered by unstable weather. One reasonably clear day would be followed by two or three days when the wind howled. Climbing without a tent, Tejas sought shelter under the snow, digging rectangular trenches about the size of a freezer. Sometimes, curled up in his bag under the surface of the glacier, he'd take out his harmonica and blow a few tunes.

By the time Tejas reached the 16,000-foot level, he was several days behind schedule and had to ration his food. The solitude, cold and incessant wind began to get to him: "I felt very vulnerable. I realized life is too short and precious to leave important things undone. I started thinking about my father. The hurt had stayed with me all these years, buried inside. I didn't want to die up there without getting in touch with him. Sixteen years without talking to my dad was too long. When I started climbing beyond 16,000 feet, tears were streaming down my cheeks."

At a tiny, wind-swept plateau at 17,200 feet, Tejas had another emotional encounter. It was from this same spot that Uemura had climbed to the top but never returned. To honor him, Tejas was carrying a Japanese flag. "It's hard to describe, but I felt his presence. It wasn't just the sounds of the storm. This is where he had perished. He was out there."

Wind continued to batter the slopes with snow. Tejas's food was running out. If the weather didn't break he'd have to go down. One morning the wind slackened. Clouds still obscured the higher slopes, but Tejas knew this might be his only chance: "I couldn't see the route, but I had guided it so often that I could sort of feel my way toward the summit. I kept reminding myself I'd turn back if the risk became too great. I had come too far to die."

As Tejas clambered onto the summit, there was no view, no distance, only his thoughts and a wall of snow blowing over Denali and out across the inviolable range. Ever so cautiously, he descended into the storm.

There were times he couldn't see beyond the reach of his ice ax. With no visibility, no sense of depth or direction, he stumbled blindly toward the 11,000-foot level, fully aware that the storm was hiding a series of large crevasses. To tell if a crevasse crossed his path, he tossed a willow wand in front of himself. He threw it again and again, at least 3,000 times, for 3,000 steps.

Twenty-six days after he had started up, Tejas staggered back to Base Camp where a plane could pick him up. "I was at the limits of my abilities—skillwise, strengthwise, foodwise, mentally, emotionally. But we made it—me and my ladder."

Vern's reception in Anchorage was overwhelming. Strangers came up and hugged him. Kids asked for his autograph. Men in the laborers union told him that they had been saying prayers for his safe return. An entire auditorium full of people sang him happy birthday. In the midst of it all, he called his father and they spoke for the first time in 16 years.

EVEREST UNSUPPORTED AND WITHOUT SUPPLEMENTARY OXYGEN

by Alison Hargreaves

*B*ritish climber Alison Hargreaves turned heads when she soloed the six major north faces of the Alps in one summer, then followed up by pioneering a new route up Katenga in the Himalayas. Later, she became the first female to climb both Mount Everest and K2 without supplementary oxygen. In June 1995 Hargreaves accepted a commission from the British Alpine Journal to write about her Everest ascent in May. The following article, intended for a Japanese magazine, was written at K2 Base Camp and sent out by runner. Shortly after writing this piece, Hargreaves summited K2 and died on her descent during a wind storm. Some of Hargreaves's achievements are chronicled in her book A Hard Day's Summer.

‡   ‡   ‡

Diary entry, 1994: "Outside the wind is howling. The tent has not stopped flapping for the last thirty hours. The wind, trying to tear the tent to shreds is doing a good job pulling at the thin layers of cloth and striving to drag down both me and my fragile shelter. It is decision time. Either I must descend from here back to Camp 2—down the Lhotse Face in search of shelter—or make an attempt on the summit. From here, on this desolate windy cot at around 8,000 meters, I still have a long way to go. The weather is against me, but this may be my last chance and I have to try . . ."

On that attempt to climb Everest via the Western Cwm and South Col in the autumn of 1994, I had to turn back at around 8,400 meters or risk losing some fingers and toes. The decision was a calculated judgment based on what was happening to my digits. Bad weather and lack of oxygen had all combined to accentuate the onset of frostbite. With less wind and with supplementary bottled oxygen things might have been different, but this was the way I had chosen to climb Everest, and for me it was the only way.

Returning to the United Kingdom I felt empty—I had put in so much energy, both physical and mental, into carrying all my own equipment onto the mountain. But a mountain is nothing without a summit—and so far the summit had eluded me.

Finally, in the middle of March 1995, after much disappointment and refusals by expeditions to let me join them, I found an expedition—led by Russell Brice of *Himalayan Experience*—who were prepared to let me join their permit, yet were happy for me to act totally independently on the mountain above Base Camp. As before, I hoped to climb alone and without the use of supplementary oxygen. On Everest in 1994 I had given myself no more than a 5 or 10 percent chance of reaching the summit in this style—but what is a goal unless it is a distant one? This somehow seemed to make it even more challenging.

So now, finally accepted on a permit and with only two weeks to prepare before the latest arrival date in Kathmandu (when the team would be leaving for Tibet), things became frantic. In seven days the freight would be sent from London, and currently I had no money to pay for the expedition either! A few days in Switzerland on a photo shoot gave me some time to think and I returned to green and wet Scotland with renewed energy. With the help of a friend, Richard Allen, I put together equipment lists, prioritizing, and chased up various sponsors who efficiently sent crucial food and kit just in time for packing. Then the grand pack—everything crammed into plastic sealed barrels after being laid out and listed on my parents' living-room floor—and the equipment was sent off with Richard for freighting. That left me with a week to sort out everything else.

The candle was being burnt at both ends. I was still carrying on my regular daily training of running, plus the odd really long day in the mountains, while tying up last-minute paperwork, sometimes working in the office by the fax machine until the early hours of the morning. Then there were the family, children and general household duties! Finally, on the evening of March 28th, I said cheerio to my family and boarded the overnight sleeper from Scotland to London. Ben Nevis, plastered in its winter coat of snow, glistened in the evening light.

Meeting my parents in London, we crossed the city in the early hours and headed out to Heathrow. After checking my bags at the desk and wishing my parents good-bye, I boarded the plane—my second attempt on Everest was about to begin.

Kathmandu was much the same as I had left it only five months before. When I descended from Everest in the autumn I had felt empty—as if someone had ripped out my stomach. Now, with renewed energy and motivation, I was happy to be back. As we ambled down the streets from the airport to the Hotel Gauri Shankar everything was much the same as it always was, with old and the modern combined. There are now as many four-wheel-drive vehicles as rickshaws. Ringing bells and bleeping horns are still the main mode of communication, but the vehicles cooperate and thus are able to make headway along the congested roads. Wafts of aromas and smells come drifting through the windows—yes, here I was back in Kathmandu.

Within a couple of days, expedition visas were tidied up and sorted with the various government bodies, and the group, which consisted of about twelve people, boarded the flight to Lhasa. This time I was going to attempt Everest from Tibet and the north side of the mountain, which had a much harder reputation. I was excited at the prospect of a more interesting challenge! As we approached the airstrip at Lhasa the aircraft was buzzing with excitement. But within seconds this turned into disappointment as the plane started to bounce violently, and the captain tried to break the news gently that we wouldn't be going to Lhasa after all—but instead to a godforsaken place in China called Chengdu! It had been too turbulent to land, so we all consoled ourselves with the thought that perhaps tomorrow would be better. But the next day the same thing happened—and we returned again to our favorite hotel in Chengdu! When we finally touched down in Lhasa on the third day, it was to cheers and great relief. At last we were in Tibet and our adventures could begin.

Instantly I fell in love with Tibet. Its stark barrenness filled me with excitement. After boarding the jeeps to drive from the airport to the city of Lhasa itself, I jumped out at every opportunity to snap a photo and take in the ambience. There was something about the Tibetan Plateau that made me feel alive. We spent a couple of days in Lhasa acclimatizing and sightseeing at the beautiful and famous Potala Palace. Soon we were again boarding jeeps piled high with rucksacks and equipment and were on our way to the mountains. This was very different from the days of leisurely trekking necessary to penetrate most other remote mountain areas. Bouncing along dirt roads, we spent three days traveling across the Tibetan Plateau, listening to Western/Tibetan music on the tape deck, finally arriving at Base Camp bounced, battered and shaken, unacclimatized but ready for the climb. On April 11th we drove into Base Camp. I'd had an upset stomach since Lhasa and now, feeling absolutely wasted, I slumped into a shallow sleep, only to wake at our destination with a cramped and twisted back—and greatly in need of some strengthening and sobering exercise.

Within two days I was active—and happy! Over the next few days I spent long days hiking on the surrounding 6,000 meter hills above Base Camp, getting fit, acclimatizing and mentally preparing. By now I felt very comfortable sleeping at Base Camp at around 5,400 meters and was ready to make the long journey, 15 miles up, toward Advanced Base Camp. On the day I arrived I felt great, even though I had jumped to 6,400 meters. My body had been ready and coped well. However, in my excitement I found it hard to sleep and was up and wide awake at 4 A.M., trying to find things to do. Advanced Base still needed some finishing touches, and by keeping busy I was able to contribute and help toward the overall comfort and happiness of all of us.

Now that I was able to see my goal I was able to focus and start to formulate a plan of action. Over the next few days I started to move my equipment up the mountain. Above lay the angled slopes of the glacier leading to the steep slopes below the North Col. I would get up reasonably early and at around dawn, after some hot drinks and biscuits, shoulder my heavy rucksack and start the long haul up the glacier. After three such carries and a night sleeping up there, I felt in a much stronger position. So I decided to descend right back down to Base Camp, even though it was 15 miles away, for what I hoped would be a rest. One of the advantages/disadvantages of coming down from a higher to a lower altitude is the amount of energy it seems to give you. Long evenings of drinking and discussions crushed my good intentions of total rest and relaxation!

Within three days I was back at Advanced Base Camp and starting to look toward moving higher up the mountain. I knew my summit attempt would have to be made from a camp much higher than the North Col at 7,000 meters, so I worked toward getting a tent and equipment set up at around 7,600 meters. When I first arrived there I felt breathless, lethargic and exhausted. The previous day I had carried a load up to 7,400 meters, and left it there to descend back down to a more comfortable altitude.

The following day I had gone up again, with another load, to 7,400 meters. I wanted to sleep higher but needed both loads in order to set up a camp. There was no way I felt I could carry higher, descend back down and carry up the second load. If I wanted to sleep high that night, there was only one option: strap the loads together and do it in one push.

The incentive of knowing that it was wise to sleep high helped me; without that knowledge I could never have made it. The weight of the double load was too much for me but I knew my goal and slowly, slowly scrambled up toward it. Finally I arrived at an area of old campsites. Most previous platforms had been demolished by the twisting and turning of the ice layer underneath, but I was able to construct a very comfortable level area from large flat stones. Using the yards of old tent fabric strewn around I prevented the base from slipping, and secured the tent quite satisfactorily with old French rope. The site would be exposed to high winds channeling through the tunnel above the North Col. It needed to be secure.

Finally my campsite was complete. All I needed to do now was to fill a nylon stuffsack full of snow and ice to melt later into liquid in the tent, and then I could crawl into my home and make myself comfortable. First I laid out the closed-cell foam mat that I had brought along both to insulate the tent and protect it from the rock and ice underneath. Then I set about arranging all my essential equipment. Stacking comestibles on one side, along with the gas, stove and bag of snow, on the other side I put all the spare items of clothing I would need higher up: gloves, balaclavas, electric socks, etc. Then it was time to drink and sleep. With the stove constantly burning and melting snow into water, I put on more warm clothes, down suit etc., and crawled into my sleeping bag to rest.

At 7,600 meters I was totally on my own, but that evening I felt as though I was not. I was convinced that someone or something was pacing around my tent. I was frightened to open the door. I knew there couldn't be anyone there, but at least it felt friendly. I consoled myself that it was checking that everything was okay. Slowly, I was able to drift into a deep and much-needed sleep.

Now I felt totally ready for a summit attempt. Given good weather and some relaxation, I felt in a strong position to try. I returned to Advanced Base Camp and aired my thoughts to a couple of friends. The barometer was set high and, as long as the weather held and I got enough rest, it seemed as though I should make an attempt. The next couple of days I just relaxed, playing cards and Monopoly. I slept a great deal and ate and drank as much as I felt I could take.

On Thursday, May 11 I set off from camp. Leaving my tent at around 6 A.M., I quickly motored up to the North Col. Then, collecting the tent from there, I continued on up toward the camp at 7,600 meters. Today was the day to rehydrate. Tomorrow I would be going much higher and I needed to have a lot of liquid inside me to help cope with the altitude and guard against the dreaded high-altitude mountain sickness. That evening I slept well, excited at the prospect of going even higher tomorrow. I drank a load, slept a load and got some needed rest.

The next day was slow and difficult as I carried up my equipment for the night: tent, stove, gas, etc. My sack felt heavy and the higher I went it seemed to increase in weight. As I touched 8,000 meters I hit a wall and my speed reduced rapidly. The snowfield that had looked so small from below seemed to take an age. After every few steps I needed much longer to recover and I felt as if I would never reach my destination. Finally, in the late afternoon, I arrived at 8,300 meters and the site of a few other tents—camps of other groups set up by Sherpas and ready to be occupied once the climbers were ready to reach them. But where was I to camp? All available flat spots had been taken; there was not a single flat area on which to pitch my tent. I would have to start work and make one myself. I ambled round slowly, tired from the day's climb and lethargic with the altitude—but I had to make a platform. Without it I could not pitch my tent and without that I would have no essential shelter in which to spend the night.

Eventually I found an area of icy rubble on a 45-degree slope and, on my hands and knees, set about chopping the ice with my axe and moving stones with my hands to form a ledge approximately six feet long and two feet wide. Exhausted, I erected my tent and tied it off to a large boulder. At around four feet wide, the tent overhung the ledge somewhat, but the ledge was wide enough to allow me to lie flat on my foam mat, and for brewing I could sit, feet dangling, but cozy inside my tent. I was tired, overtired. Today had been an exceptionally hard day and I still had another even harder one to come. I made an effort to rehydrate and was able to force down around four liters of liquid. I tried to sleep, but without a sleeping bag (which I was unable to carry) I would nod off and every half-hour wake up shivering—and have to go through the motions again of moving every part of my body individually to get back feeling and mobility and stop my body from shaking. It was going to be a long night!

Around 2 A.M. I started to prepare to make a move. It was still dark outside so I used my headlamp torch to put on my boots and neoprene overboots with crampons attached. Around 3:30 A.M. I stepped outside into the night. It was hostile, cold and dark and I could feel the cold biting up from the ground. In these temperatures my feet would be vulnerable to frostbite. I decided to go back in my tent.

Around 4:40 A.M. I finally set off. By now it was almost light; the temperature had risen a little and I was able to move without a headlamp. I was excited. I had waited for this day a long time, and now finally I was able to have it. Fresh snow overlay the rocks, but as I climbed up the ramp toward the ridge the snow became more consolidated. And the higher I climbed the more excited I became. Around 9:30 A.M. I approached the ridge and was greeted by an amazing sight. As I looked straight across toward the steep face of Makalu and farther right to the famous summit ridges of Lhotse, I felt inspired and motivated to go on.

The traversing became a little delicate. I was very much aware that one slip would end in disaster. The blank featureless slopes beneath me would not help a stop—and every step had to be deliberate and cautious.

By midmorning I had passed the famous first and second rock steps. Once more I was on the crest of the ridge and feeling very positive. My pace was slow—but I radioed down to Base Camp and told them I felt strong and hoped to be summiting within the next couple of hours. I sensed the excitement from below—that helped to secure my positiveness—and even though every step I took became slower as I got higher, I felt more and more excited at the prospect of reaching the summit!

Around noon, having reached the top of the last rock and snow pyramid, I suddenly saw the summit. I could see the curving ridge rising gradually toward the final summit cone. Tears overcame me. Weeping with emotion I radioed down, "I can see the summit," and the next ten minutes for me were like walking on air. The snow was perfect crisp, crunchy neve, and I could sense getting there. Even though I could only make a few steps before having to stop and rest, I knew I could reach it. It was just a matter of minutes.

At 12:08 P.M., May 13, 1995, I stood on the top of Everest and, radioing down to Base Camp amongst tears from me and cheers and tears from below, I relayed my message: "To my two children Tom and Kate— I am standing on the top of the world and I love you dearly."

Leaving red silk flowers in memory of those who perished or didn't make it, I took a few photos, then turned around to start my long descent back down the mountain.

Thanks must go to all those who helped me reach the summit. Their names are too numerous to list here, but without them I could not have reached my goal.

A LIFE IN THE DAY OF A
MOUNTAINEER

by Peter Croft

*I*n the summer of 1992, Peter Croft made the second traverse, on sight and
solo, of the Minarets in California's High Sierra, climbing 16 summits, mostly
between 11,000 and 12,000 feet, in a 21.5-hour push. The exposed ridge that
links them is very complicated, and involves tedious route-finding and rock of
variable (usually poor) quality, volcanic in origin rather than the clean granite
found in most of the Sierra. Vern Clevenger and Claude Fiddler, both expert rock
climbers, made the first traverse over three days in 1982, and since Croft's solo
the traverse has been repeated only one more time, according to reports.
Considering the traffic other classic Sierra climbs receive each year, this says a
lot about the difficulty of the Minaret Traverse—not to mention the perils of
climbing it solo.

Croft, a renowned hard-rock soloist, elevated the craft to high art with his
mind-boggling ropeless ascents of long Yosemite free climbs in the '80s and early
'90s. He likewise pushed the standards of speed climbing classic big walls
(including ascents of El Capitan and Half Dome, both in one day). As celebrated
as these achievements are, he calls his solo traverse of the Minarets, "My hardest
day in the mountains."

‡   ‡   ‡

I'm itchy hot and it's a cool night here at the mountain's roots, here at the
beginning. Flat on my back at the end of the road, I'm lying still but my
mind swings back and forth, arguing. Gee: I've said it all before and heard
it all before.

Is it dangerous?

How dangerous?

Do I want it?

How much?

Around and around till I'm dizzy. These conversations used to be about good granite, known ground, home ground. But now, unless I decide against myself, I'm headed for more than a baker's dozen of rotten red-brown spires, the Minarets in California's High Sierra. Dangerous place, apparently—even the guidebook warns against it.

So here I am with a swirling head and it's getting late and I've gotta sleep. Could go south; there's granite there. Could go north—but no, I find that I want this loss of control. I want to feel very small in very deep water. I don't want to know what I'm doing, but to learn it.

I wake up 30 seconds before my alarm—12:30 A.M. Start the coffee pot and sit silently, watching while my mind percolates. Then, too soon, it's time to leave this warm place and go outside where the world hasn't started yet and everything is bigger than I am. The door of my van slamming sounds like a gong. I step into the night and a cold wind washes my head.

I'm light-footed and tripping like a toddler, trying to make my steps longer. My pack, which is bigger than I'd hoped, feels like nothing. It's sort of like a kid on my shoulders, swinging back and forth with each step. Giddyup!

My headlamp is bright, but I don't get a view. The moon's only half full and it won't rise till 2 A.M., stuck in a dusty circle of light, rising up through waves of black forest.

Round a bend a new wave of glacial air hits me. My sweat turns nasty on me and I tense my muscles, but I feel great, like shifting gears or something. No longer a climber. I'm a small boy afraid of the dark but faced with it. The half moon's up, shedding enough icy light to show me the line of rotting black fangs on the skyline. I'm thrilled to be here because all I can do is my best and if that's not enough I'll still have gone through so many layers of myself that I'll remember it forever. This adventure is like a life and I feel very young.

But I'm still in the dark when the trail bends at the lake and I lose my way and make mistakes that only a child would make. So I backtrack and crisscross and find a gully that leads to a notch between the first two peaks. When I get there a thin strip of pumpkin orange is on the horizon and I get that little rush that the non-nocturnal get when they realize night isn't permanent. My headlamp makes my head hurt.

Still too dark for the tricky first tower so I go up the easy second and then back. Now it seems incredible that I can see long distances; but I still get lost, find the climbing hard and only discover the right way up on the way down. It's fully light now and I take awkward long steps down the gully to look for my gray pack on the gray rocks. From there, up and around on more gullies and terraces to the small icefield that I had hoped would be smaller, and which leads to the col. I can't really afford the time and bloody hands it would take to cut steps with a rock, so I hand traverse the upper ice edge to a point where I can get lost on the loose north face of Peak 3. I try to go daintily, but I'm a hunchback with a backpack so the most I can do, it seems, is poke my ostrich head way in the back of corners and, when I can, stuff my hands two feet deep to equalize the pressure on the shaky flakes. I reach the ridge crest and my eyes plunge down a waterfall of exposure. From the top, I can see where I'm going, a puzzle just starting to make sense.

Now there's a peak to the south, but the main ridge swoops around north and that's where I'm headed. The day and I are too young to be conservative, though, so my pack gets shed like homework and I talus-run to Peak 4 and back in no time. Now the peaks go way up north and I sideswipe more talus to puzzle out Peak 5. I find the wrong way and hurry up it, cursing the guidebooks for undergrading and myself for climbing poorly. At the summit area I look across a heartbreak gap to a slightly higher top, eddies of vertigo swirling between. To backtrack and do it right is a very big detour and the shortcut is so short a cut.

I downclimb to the notch like a cat down a tree and hand traverse on little leaning ledges. The exposure really bugs me and it feels as if my whole spinal cord is curling up like a monkey tail. Have to be careful. At the summit I stop gulping, since I can see the way down isn't nearly as bad.

At Iceberg Lake, I dump my pack, drink all I can hold, and sidetrack a bit to Peak 6, seeing mountain varmints swarming through a boulderfield like it was Swiss cheese.

Back at the lake I fill two water bottles, and consider. The next three peaks are the biggest and I've done a lot to get where I am. I know what I want from life, though, and get on with it. I get to the airy slot between Clyde and Eichorn. I'm on edge because there are so many ways to go and everywhere in these dragon-back peaks the scales are shedding. Clyde is the highest and when I get there, I can see where I've come from, but the future is getting more complex as both the day and I get older. I cross over to Peak 9, toe-shuffling a narrow ledge on this skyscraper, not knowing if my pack will overbalance me.

Now I'm faced with one more sidetrack—Michael Minaret, second highest in the group. I can't ignore it even though it's off the main ridge. I stash my pack with the rope inside—stupid, stupid—and spend way too long scrabbling down and then over fins and into gullies just getting to the spire, climbing way harder than it should be. Steep bulges bully me off tight until I find an overhanging flaky finger crack. I scratch away with frightened claws at loose pebbles, so I can grab deeper, then before my hands can sweat, pop a foot way out left and swing into a layback and go. Eventually, I settle into a pace and even peer over and smile at the abyss. At the top I crow like a rooster and it echoes back in a hundred voices.

My pack feels like home when I reach it and again I drink all I can, and eat. It's early afternoon and I haven't stopped for 14 hours. My momentum is wavering and I enter a midday crisis. Every incident has put little chinks in my armor. I'm a long way from totally shattered but I can feel the exposure is seeping through the cracks. From here I could escape relatively easily. In four hours I could be back at the campground. The way ahead is a crazy test of spires that just get wilder and wilder, like a mangy set of claws, needle-sharp and bending this way and that. Is this what I really want? As a kid swimming in the ocean I was okay as long as I could see the bottom. If not, I always got a hollow feeling and my

The Minaret Traverse in California's High Sierra roughly follows the jagged skyline in this photo, hitting every summit. Croft soloed the entire traverse in under 22 hours.
PHOTO BY JOHN MOYNIER

nuts would crowd up into my guts and I couldn't breathe properly. As I squint over in the direction my life might take I feel some of that hollowness. Well, what have I come for? I had felt a bit too much in control lately and wanted to get all wide-eyed again. So now I know. It's an amazingly calm powerful thrill to enter water this deep.

I feel more certain of myself. I still make mistakes and get lost, but now I realize that this is part of life. At times, the very best option is a lousy one but is the way to go. I reach a very steep section and have to cross. Better hold on tight because that's a big loose block and I really want to step on it. The block dives out and my body swings sideways, right foot darting into a crack like a swallow.

The smallest spire is the hardest and steepest and the only place I belay myself. I only have a few pieces of gear and nothing is very good. As I climb the summit block against rope drag I realize my silly self-belay is about as much good as an upside-down toprope.

The sun's getting lower and I'm getting older. Have to watch myself now, and use my experience to find a canny way up. So I drop down a long gully and ditch most of my stuff on a great white rock. I go over a couple of summits to reach the main one, zigzagging to avoid difficulties that would have been easy this morning when I was young. Doddering a bit on the way down, I rappel rather than make a five-minute detour. The endurance that I once thought inexhaustible is fading.

I may be too tired. I don't know if I can . . . I fiddle with the laces of my climbing shoes. The sun is fluttering close to the horizon. One more peak, the last. I just want to rest, though. I can feel the cold of the coming blackness. Cuts and scrapes are all over me. My sunset is very near but the last peak obscures it. I could walk away now but then I would know my love of adventure wasn't strong enough. Promises and decisions I've made in my long, long life this day come surging back. I double-knot my laces and creak to my feet with a lopsided smile, actually sort of surprised at the sudden wave of energy I get, like a sunburst before sunset. With a wondering mind, I climb the face up a wandering route and reach the ridge crest a long way from the top. A bald arete halts me for a minute, then I hand traverse up, feet smearing on ripples, and then it's easy and then it's the top. I raise myself like an old bear onto my tired legs and look north. A deep pass below me and more mountains going away until I can't see them anymore. Now is my sunset and it's beautiful and sad. I still have to get down, but it's over now. I'm happy and satisfied in a way that makes me feel even older.

I stay very watchful on the descent, carefully cleaning the soles of my

Another time, another place. . . . For years, Peter Croft has been soloing classic Yosemite cracks such as Tips (5.12). PHOTO BY GREG EPPERSON

shoes when they pick up grit. And then I'm down and the tension floods out through my pores. I slip on my walking shoes and they feel like dessert. I begin the long walk out to the end, first on ice, then rocks, then on a faint trail that grows and grows. And then it's night and it's down through those black waves that looked different a lifetime ago. The path that was so well defined looks indistinct now, my rubber legs casting about in the dark for solid ground. My headlamp is still bright as ever but I'm not and I totter clean off the John Muir Superhighway. I sway south through the forest, then find the path again. I have to be careful. I have to get down, then I can sleep.

Little thought-bits are swirling around when I reach the campground. The bright lights make me stagger a bit on the way to put my load down. In the van, I roll down the road, sipping coffee and making movies in my head, reliving the essence of a long, long day.

I go to bed like an old man, and sleep like a baby.

FITZROY: SOLO ON THE NORTH PILLAR

Renato Casarotto

P *atagonia is situated in the southern tip of Argentina and presents some of the greatest climbing challenges on the planet, including massive Fitzroy (11,289) and needle-like Cerro Torre (10,262). Streaming off the Patagonian ice caps, treacherous winds and snow rip the granite walls resulting in a success rate lower than virtually any other distinguished climbing region—a remarkable statistic considering only skilled professionals dare climb there at all. To scale one of the range's formidable peaks is a landmark achievement for any climber's career. To solo a new route on such peaks—as Renato Casarotto describes in the following story—is, according to Patagonian veteran Nigel Hammonds, "like challenging the Devil in hell." Renato Casarotto did so—and won.*

‡   ‡   ‡

In January of 1978 I went to Patagonia with the Morbengo Section of the Italian Alpine Club. Our objective was the northwest face of Fitzroy. As we approached the mountain, however, we realized that the few days at our disposal were not enough time to attempt this wall. We turned to the north pillar, which presented an easier approach; but hurricane winds and snow, plus the difficulty of the route, forced us to withdraw. This first contact with wild and primitive Patagonia fascinated me to the point that I had to return as soon as possible.

In April of the same year some friends from Bermio showed keen interest in my plan, and the second expedition was under way. At the beginning it involved the participants alone, but soon an official cloak was given and the project and was named The Expedition Contea CAI Bermio-Fitzroy 1978–1979. The climbers were Luigi Zen, Giovanni Mafori and myself as putative leader. My wife offered to handle the logistics, and completed the team.

Finally on November 8, 1978, the expedition left Italy for Buenos Aires. From there, having completed the bureaucratic formalities, we flew to Rio Gallegos, and from there, by truck, we reached Fitzroy National Park. On November 20 we departed for Base Camp, eight miles distant, using the mules of the local constabulary as beasts of burden. We were so inspired by the good weather and the stupendous view of the mountain that, having rapidly established Base Camp, we departed immediately for Advanced Base Camp. As is customary for expeditions in Patagonia, we excavated an ice cave for an equipment depot and a refuge in case of bad weather.

On December 6 the unforeseen happened; the other two climbers quit the expedition. Brutal winds and the mile-high wall had destroyed their enthusiasm. Words were useless to convince them to give it a try. Thus my wife and I remained alone to carry on as best we could. I was determined to try and solo our objective, the north pillar, an untried route. My only solo experience was from the previous year, on the north face of Huascaran Norte in the Peruvian Andes.

The weather worsened rapidly and with such intensity that we had to move Base Camp since the wind had demolished the tent. We were able to organize ourselves in a log cabin, transporting there with hard work all the gear. Notwithstanding the bad weather, I succeeded in climbing back up as far as the notch between the pillar and the peak Val del Biois, ascending a couloir of mixed ice, snow and rock for about 1,000 feet. Here I pitched a tent to which I would return every night in order to climb back up along the fixed ropes the following day.

Since an improvement in the weather was not foreseen, I decided to see how far I could proceed safely. I managed 200 feet and immediately became aware of how hard it was to climb in such conditions, with the violent wind that struck from every side, the stinging and torturous snow, and fingertips that turned to ice when I climbed bare-handed. To ensure some means of retreat, I decided to fix the greater part of the climb.

Only on January 1, 1979, did the conditions improve enough to let me resume the ascent. As in my preceding solo climb, I used a system of dynamic self-belays to guarantee my safety. I climbed thus for 500 feet along dihedrals, cracks and chimneys, encountering severe free climbing. The following day I proceeded for another 500 feet, reaching, always with great difficulty, the top of an enormous dihedral.

The third day the sky was covered and the wind rose, rendering progress slow. I succeeded in gaining only 350 feet up the ever-present cracks and chimneys that characterize this wall. The pitch was stupendous. If it had not been for the ice that in places completely filled the cracks, I might have climbed it entirely free. One thing that struck me was the absolute absence of sharp edges usually found in granite. I observed how on this pillar the violent wind and the formation of ice had smoothed the surface to the texture of polished marble.

On January 4, following the edge of the east corner of the pillar for 500 feet, I climbed into a dihedral and thence, having ascended numerous cracks and the final steps, I reached the summit of the north pillar at a little less than 10,000 feet. From there I descended to the bivouac tent. During the night bad weather returned. I remained where I was for a full day, hoping the winds might die off.

It was actually better on January 6. I departed at seven o'clock in the morning, armed with a movie and a still camera, hoping to ascend to the summit of Fitzroy, but it took so long to replace some of the fixed ropes and to document the climb that I did not get to the top of the pillar until late afternoon. I began the traverse to gain the face of the main summit, finding unforeseen difficulties, which included three arduous pendulums. I climbed late into the night by the light of my headlamp, battered by the wind and falling ice. Seeing that the cold of night did not keep ice from falling, I descended into the notch between the pillar and the main summit. Toward dawn a strong, wet wind rapidly covered the rock with verglas. At dawn I began the descent, overcoming almost insuperable difficulties to reach the bivouac tent.

After making radio contact with my wife, I continued on down to Base Camp, where continual stormy weather forced me into inactivity. On January 17, I climbed back up anew to the base of the pillar, where I found the tent destroyed. I prepared as best I could to pass the night. The following day I proceeded on toward the summit of the pillar, repairing some ropes frayed by the wind. This time as well, along the face of the main summit, I had to work till late at night on account of the damage caused by bad weather. It was very late when I descended to my tentless bivouac in the notch. Toward dawn I regained my high point and thence I followed numerous cracks and dihedrals with the greatest difficulties yet encountered because the walls were completely covered with snow and ice. Finally, on the afternoon of January 19, I gained the summit. Having taken the ritual photographs, I hastened to descend and in the afternoon of the following day I returned to the mini Base Camp and to my wife.

In going over these notes, I cannot avoid comparing technical considerations with personal ones. From a strictly mountaineering point of view, I can say that in ten active years I had never lived through such a total experience. On this wall I had to overcome extreme technical difficulties under the most continuous foul weather. The equipment and food I had were what is usually used on Alpine climbs, but I also had impermeable Gore-Tex clothing. This adventure confirmed in my mind that to succeed in ascents of noteworthy difficulty it is indispensable to integrate oneself into the surroundings. That is to say that one must know how to determine the most propitious conditions for the ascent so that one's physical and psychological energies are not dissipated in long waits.

To my wife, who was infinitely patient and understanding, I dedicate the summit of the north pillar of Fitzroy. From now on I shall call it the Goretta Pillar.

SOLO ON CLOGGY

by Wilfrid Noyce

S *olo on Cloggy," taken from Wilfrid Noyce's book* Mountains and Men *and featured here, describes a ropeless ascent of* Curving Crack (5.7) *at Clogwyn du'r Arddu, the spiritual home of British rock climbing. Written in 1947, Noyce's account reflects an era when intellectuals sought the "meaning" of serious physical endeavors by casting them into mythical terms. And yet— try as he did—all the myths from all the ages could not tell Wilfrid Noyce what he'd experienced when "mind and body combined." Ultimately, trying to knead the mojo of soloing into words is like trying to bottle lightning. Likewise, contrasting a keenly personal solo experience with the trials of Jason, for instance, is asking the Argonaut to connect the dots on your own experience. No harm in trying—but in the end the best a soloer can do is lay back on the grass and wonder, and maybe later offer up a few thoughts and feelings.*

‡ ‡ ‡

It must have been that fascination, overmastering and fatal as was ever the blindness that took Pentheus to his doom among the Bacchae, which led me once to the steepest cliff in Wales. The sense of intimacy that possesses the solitary had become, it may be, an infatuation; more and more I had thought that I might presume, if my love be kind, until it seemed that there was no liberty that I could not take. It was a May morning of 1942, and I was under the precipice of Clogwyn du'r Arddu. I had stepped from bright sun into the slanting shadow of the eastern buttress. I blinked up at it, at the row of vertical cracks that split it. On the right I could see the *Curving Crack* that Colin Kirkus, I knew, had climbed with Alf Bridge.

The day was warm, the rocks dry and the moss peeled from them under a rubber shoe. I started up the first layback crack; why, I could not tell. There was no sense in trying such a climb. I was tasting simply a physical pleasure—why does the small boy buy an ice cream when he has pennies about him? My legs were arched, feet pressed against the back wall. The rubbers slipped occasionally, ever so slightly. My fingers hooked around the upright crack edge. I was gaining height slowly. At the top of the first section, 30 feet above the turf, I surveyed future and past: the vertical walls of the buttress and the little ledge on which I stood. A comforting crack split the cliff above me, shaped exactly for the wedging of a human body. But it must be hard; if I could not go on, could I go back? The climber has his lesser Rubicons. I knew that infatuation was upon me; that I could not break this spell of movement, of tense wonder at my physical doing. I must go on, to watch body and mind working in their own right together. Now in self-defense I must give of the best: a poor kind of best, perhaps, if you could catalogue "bests," but one that would satisfy me for a day. The crack ahead must be a struggle; again, could I get down, was I doomed to crouch like a sheep stranded on its tuft, waiting till I starve or fall? And would it not be a pity so to fall, to end in a moment this bundle of nerve and muscle, of action begun and hope for things incomplete?

I wrestled hotly to the top of the *Curving Crack*, in a fear and a sure vowing that I could never be guilty of the like rashness again. On the grass above, I lay in the sun. I had done—what? I had done something that only I could tell. Something foolish, something that I must not repeat, but something that I felt still to have been "worth" the doing. And I could no more simplify the climb into an idiocy than into a conquest; there was more to it than that, as there must be more to any hard effort in which mind and body have combined to give. And yet if it must be set down as the one or the other, idiocy it certainly had been, and conquest never. I had by no fragment, other than the trampled grass or displaced chockstone, altered the life of that cliff. I had been allowed to scramble, a short and precarious hour, over its bare rock. I had no more conquered it than the Lilliputians conquered Gulliver, when they first walked across his chest.

ALONE ON DENALI'S SOUTH FACE

by Mark Hesse

*T*he highest mountain on the North American continent, Mount McKinley (20,320 feet, more commonly called Denali by climbers, its native Alaskan name) is one of the world's coldest mountains. Author/climber Greg Child wrote that "even halfway to the summit the climate is equivalent to that on the North Pole." As far as 4,000 feet below the mountain top, winds have driven temperatures lower than (including wind-chill factor) minus 150 degrees. Avalanches and great crevasses add to the dangers that have cost over 50 climbers their lives, and have occasioned countless rescues. The rate of frostbite is higher on Denali than perhaps any other mountain in the world. It was on the chilling south face of this killing field that Mark Hesse climbed in the footsteps of British mountaineering legends Dougal Haston and Doug Scott—alone. Not mentioned by Hesse was the remarkable detail that some dozen years before this historic solo ascent he'd nearly lost his hand in a machining accident. Apparently, Hesse didn't consider his impairment worth noting.*

‡   ‡   ‡

I was at an impasse. Seated on my pack, elbows on my knees, chin buried in the palms of my hands, I stared at the 9,000 feet of rock and ice before me. I was on the edge of the glaciated basin below the south face of Denali, one of the greatest mountain faces in North America, inspiring in beauty yet hostile, a land form on the outer extreme of the planet.

I had navigated the icefall leading to the edge of the basin in the company of mountain guide and friend Michael Covington. Michael and his party were attempting the South Buttress of the peak. Now, however, I was on my own. I had ventured out across the basin a short distance when the gravity of my plan overcame me. My ambition and determination unraveled into fear, doubt and confusion. I had backtracked to reconsider, to gain control over the emotions surging through me. Fight or flight, I had to decide.

I had long been inspired by solo climbs of big peaks. To me it represented the supreme test of climbing skill, physical endurance and mental strength. Alone, you had no partner to share the hardship, share the stress, help make those judgment calls that in mountaineering are so intuitive. But my dream of a solo ascent of the south face of Denali had manifested into monstrous seracs, imposing snow and icefields and bone chilling cold. The danger that back home I had so easily pushed to the back of my mind was now staring me in the face. Somewhere near where I now stood, two Japanese climbers had disappeared without a trace.

Despite their preoccupation with crossing a large crevasse, Michael's clients turned to observe me. They sensed my dilemma, my inner turmoil. I had heard the conversations in the tents the night before. The sanity of my plan was questioned—just as I questioned it now.

Suddenly I stood, shouldered my pack, adjusted the 12-foot aluminum pole that I had crafted to keep me from falling into hidden crevasses, and began to walk again out into the basin.

I had arrived in Alaska two weeks earlier with my brother Jon. We had tried without success to climb the West Buttress Route. While the most popular route on Denali, it remains a major challenge for any climber. It was a supreme test for Jon. Ten years before, at age 22, Jon had developed osteogenic sarcoma, a particularly virulent strain of bone cancer with a five percent survival rate. It first showed up in his right knee. Doctors amputated his leg at mid-thigh. His cancer persisted, spreading into his lungs. Again they operated, this time removing a portion of one lobe. Then yet another tumor developed in his lung, and yet again they operated. This time they gave him three months to live.

There was no medical reason why Jon's cancer went into remission, why he overcame such tremendous odds. But I knew a major factor was my brother's fierce tenacity and his refusal to let go of life. Jon was not just a cancer survivor, he was a victor. And he emerged from his battle stronger than ever.

Jon had always loved to climb and saw no reason why he couldn't continue. However, after reaching 11,000 feet we had elected to go down.

His custom designed outriggers where not working well enough on steep terrain and hard ice to safely go higher. The weather had also been brutally windy and cold, and Jon could not risk frostbite in the one leg he had left. While it was a bitter disappointment, the fact that Jon had gotten as high as he did was a great accomplishment. The summit was not as important as the attempt. It was the life force of dreams and the pursuit of them that had kept Jon alive.

The huge southern flank of Denali is split into two parts: the southwest face and south face; the dividing feature between them is the famed Cassin Ridge. The south face was first climbed in 1967 by an American team. Over the course of one month they fixed 7,000 feet of rope and established multiple camps. Their route, the American Direct, was a huge accomplishment for its time. In 1976, Dougal Haston and Doug Scott, fresh from their successful climb of the Southwest Face of Mount Everest, made the second ascent of the face via a major variation to the American Direct. They climbed alpine style, always moving up, in a single six-and-a-half day effort. In the years that followed the south face was climbed twice. A Japanese team successfully completed the American Direct route in 1977 via a new variation on the lower part of the mountain. Three years latter, a Slovakian team climbed a new route between the American Direct and the South Buttress.

I had climbed the Cassin Ridge two years earlier with my good friend Chris Reveley. While on the Cassin I had looked closely at the south face. The image of this tremendous wall had stayed with me until, like a seed, it matured into my ambition to follow in Scott and Haston's footsteps, alone.

I was standing in the bergschrund at the base of the my route when I heard the ominous sound of falling snow and ice. The avalanche filled the sky and tons of frozen detritus swept out across the basin. After leaving Michael's company I had kept to the east side of the valley, moving as quickly as the weight of my pack would allow. I had reached the safety of the bergschrund only moments before the tremendous icefield halfway up the face, known to climbers as Big Bertha, released. I was safe but shaken. Never had I been so close to so large an avalanche. As I shoveled out a platform for my tent I turned often to search for Michael's party, just to catch a glimpse of other people, regardless of how distant, and gain slight comfort.

The following morning I forced myself from my sleeping bag as early as possible. The weather was stable. With the glacier and its hidden crevasses behind me, I could now focus on the climb. I had prepared for the expansive icefields that loomed overhead for months, running hills and more hills, punishing my legs and lungs into shape. A short step over the bergschrund and I was up and away.

The snow that covered the ice was unconsolidated and, consequently, the climbing was slow and tedious. My apprehension and doubt dissipated into the rare arctic air as the enormity of the climb was reduced to individual movements. One ax placement, then another. A kick of a crampon, a step up, another kick. A routine repeated over and over separated by rhythmic breaths. I climbed throughout the day, reaching the first rock band late in the afternoon. I had anticipated difficulty in finding bivouac spots on the lower half of the route. As I expected, what ledges there were were encased in ice. I located a small rocky outcrop and after two hours of torturous chopping I managed to fashion a small trench. It would be my home for the night. As the sun set I peered out across the arctic wasteland, the protection of my sleeping bag and bivy sack seeming ever so meager.

Early the next day I climbed back onto the ice. The higher I climbed the more the glacier fell away below me. Continuous frontpointing with my heavy pack worked me into a state of severe physical and mental exhaustion. The afternoon of my second day found me scrambling around on steep rock and ice at 14,000 feet, again searching for a ledge to situate myself on for the night. After some difficult mixed climbing I gained a small bench and again began once more to hack out a ledge.

I rose the following morning still tired. My night's sleep had done little to ease the strain of the previous day. I felt anxious about the next section of the icefield. It was entirely swept free of snow and the ice was bullet hard. After 300 feet of climbing I began for the first time to question my endurance. My calves ached and my crampon placements grew sloppy. Then my mind seized, locked up with the thought of losing it and falling off into the void. I escaped onto a rockband searching for relief. I spent the next several hours belaying myself and hauling my pack up a near vertical crack system. I finally reached a ledge at the edge of the icefield, my confidence in tatters. I then began to contemplate the extraordinary position I had put myself in.

I had expected to complete the climb in four or five days, approximately the same time that Chris and I had taken on the Cassin Ridge. Based upon my progress, I now guessed that it might take me two to three days longer. Because of my limited supplies, this meant I would not be able to sit out a major storm should one occur. I was close to the point of no return, where a retreat down the face would simply be impossible. The next section of the route involved a traverse across steep ice into a narrow couloir. A half hour passed, then another hour—but I did not move, locked in indecision.

In much the same fashion that I had ventured out onto the glacier three days before, I collected myself and moved out onto the ice. Never had I felt so extended on a climb. Yet I could not turn from the challenges above. As I began climbing again my determination and confidence returned. The further out I climbed the more the couloir above came into view. Despite its steep angle, it was choked with snow. A roped traverse brought me to the base of the couloir. I chopped out a small bivy ledge and settled in for the night. The evening air was still. In the fading sunlight the peaks presented themselves in divine grandeur. I was beginning to look forward to this time of day when I could gaze out across the landscape in awe. My isolation and fatigue seemed only to magnify its beauty like an elixir working its magic.

The following morning was magnificent, clear and sunny. It provided a tremendous boost, warming my mind and body. Without hesitation I began climbing. After 500 feet the couloir steepened into a near vertical headwall. At the top I found a large platform. I recognized it immediately as the very spot which Haston and Scott wrote about, where they spent a horrific night ravaged by the wind. These two legendary Himalayan climbers described it as one of the worst experiences that either of them had spent in the mountains. I was far more fortunate.

The spiral couloir branched out left from the platform and presented the most difficult climbing I'd yet encountered on the route. Full of hard, brittle ice, it steepened radically at the top. I attacked it full on, reaching a snowy knife-edged ridge close to total exhaustion. I rested briefly then continued climbing in the fading light of the day. The air grew perfectly still; there was not a breath of wind. The mountain was afire in alpenglow. I was suddenly overcome with a feeling of tremendous peace the likes of which I had never felt before in the mountains. A window to my soul had opened up and the beauty of this harsh wilderness was rushing in. I reached a large overhanging boulder and climbed under it for the night. It grew horribly cold. I later learned from a team on the West Buttress that the air temperature that evening dropped to minus 50 F. Who knows to what ungodly depths it fell later that night!

I slept late into the next day waiting until the sun was fully upon me before crawling from my frozen sack. I elected to climb up to the large triangular shaped rock buttress at 16,800 feet rather than traverse out across the top of Big Bertha. The climbing proved difficult in sections but engaging. As I meandered in and out of the rocks on the ice my ascent began to take on a new perspective. The difficult ground was behind me and success seemed less a dream and more a possibility. The buttress gave me protection enough to set up my tent for the first time since I began climbing.

The next day I traversed across the face to rejoin the Scott and Haston line which follows the wide couloir on the upper wall to the summit. The snow was firm and in excellent condition. After a full day of climbing I erected my tent in a shallow crevasse at 17,500 feet. Just before sundown, as I was finishing my dinner, I heard the drone of an engine. I searched the sky and spotted a plane flying slowly above the Kahiltna Glacier toward the face. The plane circled several thousand feet below me, then departed as it had come. I recognized the craft. It was Doug Geeting, the pilot who had flown Jon and me in. He was checking on my progress after dropping off a team of hopeful climbers on the glacier. His brief visit amplified the sense of isolation that I now felt. I was not just soloing the peak without a partner. I had severed all ties with mankind.

I had hoped to reach the summit the following day. The climb, however, was taking its toll. I was severely depleted from days of continuous toil on the mountain. The altitude was now robbing me of all opportunities to recuperate. What I thought was going to be an easy day turned into a trying one. I reached 19,200 feet before I was overcome with exhaustion. I bivouacked on a small ledge with everything on save my crampons. The severe cold seemed to enter through every pore, penetrating deep into my body. For the first time the possibility of freezing to death in the night entered my mind. Never had I felt so utterly vulnerable!

I awoke the next day to a voice from somewhere inside me. "Get up! Get up, Mark! Get going! You're going to die if you don't!" It was my brother's voice! It was Jon waking me from my half conscious, half-frozen state. I opened my eyes to clouds and driving snow. I was covered in spindrift. A storm had developed during the night. It was as if my challenge on the summit had awakened a wrathful monster. A terrible fear welled up inside me. I had to reach the top today and get down. I had overstayed my visit and it was now or never. Within minutes I was off the ledge and out onto the face. I could see absolutely nothing as I front-pointed up the couloir. Up and up I climbed into the thick of the storm without any visibility whatsoever. After what seemed like eternity the slope suddenly steepened—and then I found myself standing in the clouds. I could go no higher. Then I saw it, just a few meters away, the very place where Chris and I had stood so proudly a few years before. I took one deep breath, quickly located the route down, and immediately began my descent. On familiar ground at last. It was still a long way back but I knew the way well. I was on the home stretch!

Tears welled into my eyes as I scrambled with abandon down from the top of North America, exhausted and frozen by the storm. I was immensely proud, yes. I had pulled it off, a great personal victory, a dream come true. What more could I ask from life. Yet it was so much more. I hadn't conquered the mountain, far from it. I had engaged it, mentally and physically, in a profound way. I was leaving this place with a gift far greater than vainglorious pride and I knew that it would be a long time before I would truly descend from the heights to which the mountain had taken me.

STICKEEN

By John Muir

*M*uir's expedition across the icy wilderness of southern Alaska in 1880 *taught him about more than just glaciers and mountain travel.* *It taught him about our fellow animal companions. We are certain* *of our human intelligence when surviving feats of life and death. Courage is* *intelligence expressed. But we so often gloss over the intelligence of our mortal* *friends here on earth—namely animals of all species. If not realized, there is danger* *in bypassing invaluable partnerships of the living kind. This is a story about a* *solo effort across a glacier with an unlikely partner—a mutt named Stickeen. A* *dangerous and heroic solo climb? By no means. But anyone who's climbed alone* *in the mountains, or is fascinated by the topic, should find something enchanting* *in the following story.*

‡   ‡   ‡

In the summer of 1880 I set out from Fort Wrangel in a canoe to continue the exploration of the icy region of southeastern Alaska, begun in the fall of 1879. After the necessary provisions, blankets, etc., had been collected and stowed away, and my Indian crew were in their places ready to start, while a crowd of their relatives and friends on the wharf were bidding them good-bye and good-luck, my companion, the Rev. S. H. Young, for whom we were waiting, at last came aboard, followed by a little black dog that immediately made himself at home by curling up in a hollow among the baggage. I like dogs, but this one seemed so small and worthless that I objected to his going, and asked the missionary why he was taking him.

"Such a little helpless creature will only be in the way," I said; "you had better pass him up to the Indian boys on the wharf, to be taken home to play with the children. This trip is not likely to be good for toy-dogs. The poor silly thing will be in rain and snow for weeks or months, and will require care like a baby."

But his master assured me that he would be no trouble at all; that he was a perfect wonder of a dog, could endure cold and hunger like a bear, swim like a seal and was wondrous wise and cunning, etc., making out a list of virtues to show he might be the most interesting member of the party.

Nobody could hope to unravel the lines of his ancestry. In all the wonderfully mixed and varied dog-tribe I never saw any creature very much like him, though in some of his sly, soft, gliding motions and gestures he brought the fox to mind. He was short-legged and bunchy-bodied, and his hair, though smooth, was long and silky and slightly waved, so that when the wind was at his back it ruffled, making him look shaggy. At first sight his only noticeable feature was his fine tail, which was about as airy and shady as a squirrel's, and was carried curling forward almost to his nose. On closer inspection you might notice his thin sensitive ears, and sharp eyes with cunning tan spots above them. Mr. Young told me that when the little fellow was a pup about the size of a woodrat he was presented to his wife by an Irish prospector at Sitka, and that on his arrival at Fort Wrangel he was adopted with enthusiasm by the Stickeen Indians as a sort of new good luck totem, was named "Stickeen" for the tribe, and became a universal favorite; petted, protected, and admired wherever he went, and regarded as a mysterious fountain of wisdom.

On our trip he soon proved himself a queer character—odd, concealed, independent, keeping invincibly quiet, and doing many little puzzling things that piqued my curiosity. As we sailed week after week through the long intricate channels and inlets among the innumerable islands and mountains of the coast, he spent most of the dull days in sluggish ease, motionless, and apparently as unobserving as if in deep sleep. But I discovered that somehow he always knew what was going on. When the Indians were about to shoot at ducks or seals, or when anything along the shore was exciting our attention, he would rest his chin on the edge of the canoe and calmly look out like a dreamy-eyed tourist. And when he heard us talking about making a landing, he immediately roused himself to see what sort of a place we were coming to, and made ready to jump overboard and swim ashore as soon as the canoe neared the beach.

Then, with a vigorous shake to get rid of the brine in his hair, he ran into the woods to hunt small game. But though always the first out of the canoe, he was always the last to get into it. When we were ready to start he could never be found, and refused to come to our call. We soon found out, however, that though we could not see him at such times, he saw us, and from the cover of the briers and huckleberry bushes in the fringe of the woods was watching the canoe with wary eye. For as soon as we were fairly off he came trotting down the beach, plunged into the surf, and swam after us, knowing well that we would cease rowing and take him in. When the contrary little vagabond came alongside, he was lifted by the neck, held at arm's length a moment to drip, and dropped aboard. We tried to cure him of this trick by compelling him to swim a long way, as if we had a mind to abandon him; but this did no good: the longer the swim the better he seemed to like it.

Though capable of great idleness, he never failed to be ready for all sorts of adventures and excursions. One pitch-dark rainy night we landed about ten o'clock at the mouth of a salmon stream when the water was phosphorescent. The salmon were running, and the myriad fins of the onrushing multitude were churning all the stream into a silvery glow, wonderfully beautiful and impressive in the ebony darkness. To get a good view of the show I set out with one of the Indians and sailed up through the midst of it to the foot of a rapid about half a mile from camp, where the swift current dashing over rocks made the luminous glow most glorious. Happening to look back down the stream, while the Indian was catching a few of the struggling fish, I saw a long spreading fan of light like the tail of a comet, which we thought must be made by some big strange animal that was pursuing us. On it came with its magnificent train, until we imagined we could see the monster's head and eyes; but it was only Stickeen, who, finding I had left the camp, came swimming after me to see what was up.

When we camped early, the best hunter of the crew usually went to the woods for a deer, and Stickeen was sure to be at his heels, provided I had not gone out. For, strange to say, though I never carried a gun, he always followed me, forsaking the hunter and even his master to share my wanderings. The days that were too stormy for sailing I spent in the woods, or on the adjacent mountains, wherever my studies called me; and Stickeen always insisted on going with me, however wild the weather, gliding like a fox through dripping huckleberry bushes and thorny tangles of panax and rubus, scarce stirring their rain-laden leaves; wading and wallowing through snow, swimming icy streams, skipping over logs and rocks and the crevasses of glaciers with the patience and endurance of a determined mountaineer, never tiring or getting discouraged. Once he followed me over a glacier the surface of which was so crusty and rough that it cut his feet until every step was marked with blood; but he trotted on with Indian fortitude until I noticed his red track, and, taking pity on him, made him a set of moccasins out of a handkerchief. However great his troubles he never asked help or made any complaint, as if, like a philosopher, he had learned that without hard work and suffering there could be no pleasure worth having.

Yet none of us was able to make out what Stickeen was really good for. He seemed to meet danger and hardships without anything like reason, insisted on having his own way, never obeyed an order, and the hunter could never set him on anything, or make him fetch the birds he shot. His equanimity was so steady it seemed due to want of feeling; ordinary storms were pleasures to him, and as for mere rain, he flourished in it like a vegetable. No matter what advances you might make, scarce a glance or a tail-wag would you get for your pains. But though he was apparently as cold as a glacier and about as impervious to fun, I tried hard to make his acquaintance, guessing there must something worthwhile hidden beneath so much courage, endurance, and love of wild-weathery adventure. No super-annulated mastiff or bulldog grown old in office surpassed this fluffy midget in stoic dignity. He sometimes reminded me of a small, squat, unshakable desert cactus. For he never displayed a single trace of the merry, tricksy, elfish fun of the terriers and collies that we all know, nor of their touching affection and devotion. Like children, most small dogs beg to be loved and allowed to love: but Stickeen seemed a very Diogenes, asking only to be let alone: a true child of the wilderness, holding the even tenor of his hidden life with the silence and serenity of nature. His strength of character lay in his eyes. They looked as old as the hills, and as young, and as wild. I never tired of looking into them: it was like looking into a landscape; but they were small and rather deep set, and had no explaining lines around them to give out particulars. I was accustomed to look into the faces of plants and animals, and I watched the little sphinx more and more keenly as an interesting study. But there is no estimating the wit and wisdom concealed and latent in our lower fellow mortals until made manifest by profound experiences; for it is through suffering that dogs as well as saints are developed and made perfect.

After exploring the Sumdum and Tahkoo fiords and their glaciers, we sailed through Stephen's Passage into Lynn Canal and thence through

Icy Strait into Cross Sound, searching for unexplored inlets leading toward the great fountain icefields of the Fairweather Range. Here, while the tide was in our favor, we were accompanied by a fleet of icebergs drifting out to the ocean from Glacier Bay. Slowly we paddled around Vanconver's Point, Wimbledon, our frail canoe tossed like a feather on the massive heaving swells coming in past Cape Spenser. For miles the sound is bounded by precipitous mural cliffs, which, lashed with wave-spray and their heads hidden in clouds, looked terribly threatening and stern. Had our canoe been crushed or upset we could have made no landing here, for the cliffs, as high as those of Yosemite, sink sheer into deep water. Eagerly we scanned the wall on the north side for the first sign of an opening fiord or harbor, all of us anxious except Stickeen, who dozed in peace or gazed dreamily at the tremendous precipices when he heard us talking about them. At length we made the joyful discovery of the mouth of the inlet now called "Taylor Bay," and about five o'clock reached the head of it and encamped in a spruce grove near the front of a large glacier.

While camp was being made, Joe the hunter climbed the mountain wall on the east side of the fiord in pursuit of wild goats, while Mr. Young and I went to the glacier. We found that it is separated from the waters of the inlet by a tidewashed moraine, and extends, an abrupt barrier, all the way across from wall to wall of the inlet, a distance of about three miles. But our most interesting discovery was that it had recently advanced, though again slightly receding. A portion of the terminal moraine had been plowed up and shoved forward, uprooting and overwhelming the woods on the east side. Many of the trees were down and buried, or nearly so, others were leaning away from the ice-cliffs, ready to fall, and some stood erect, with the bottom of the ice plow still beneath their roots and its lofty crystal spires towering high above their tops. The spectacle presented by these century-old trees standing close beside a spiry wall of ice, with their branches almost touching it, was most novel and striking. And when I climbed around the front, and a little way up the west side of the glacier, I found that it had swelled and increased in height and width in accordance with its advance, and carried away the outer ranks of trees on its bank.

On our way back to camp after these first observations I planned a far-and-wide excursion for the morrow. I awoke early, called not only by the glacier, which had been on my mind all night, but by a grand floodstorm. The wind was blowing a gale from the north and the rain was flying with the clouds in a wide passionate horizontal flood, as if it were all passing over the country instead of falling on it. The main perennial streams were booming high above their banks, and hundreds of new ones, roaring like the sea, almost covered the lofty gray walls of the inlet with white cascades and falls. I had intended making a cup of coffee and getting something like a breakfast before starting, but when I heard the storm and looked out I made haste to join it; for many of Nature's finest lessons are to be found in her storms, and if careful to keep in right relations with them, we may go safely abroad with them, rejoicing in the grandeur and beauty of their works and ways, and chanting with the old Norsemen, "The blast of the tempest aids our oars, the hurricane is our servant and drives us whither we wish to go." So, omitting breakfast, I put a piece of bread in my pocket and hurried away.

Mr. Young and the Indians were asleep, and so, I hoped, was Stickeen; but I had not gone a dozen rods before he left his bed in the tent and came boring through the blast after me. That a man should welcome storms for their exhilarating music and motion, and go forth to see God making landscapes, is reasonable enough; but what fascination could there be in such tremendous weather for a dog? Surely nothing akin to human enthusiasm for scenery or geology. Anyhow, on he came, breakfastless, through the choking blast. I stopped and did my best to turn him back. "Now don't," I said, shouting to make myself heard in the storm, "now don't, Stickeen. What has got into your queer noodle now? You must be daft. This wild day has nothing for you. There is no game abroad, nothing but weather. Go back to camp and keep warm, get a good breakfast with your master, and be sensible for once. I can't carry you all day or feed you, and this storm will kill you."

But Nature, it seems, was at the bottom of the affair, and she gains her ends with dogs as well as with men, making us do as she likes, shoving and pulling us along her ways, however rough, all but killing us at times in getting her lessons driven hard home. After I had stopped again and again, shouting good warning advice, I saw that he was not to be shaken off; as well might the earth try to shake off the moon. I had once led his master into trouble, when he fell on one of the topmost jags of a mountain and dislocated his arm; now the turn of his humble companion was coming. The pitiful little wanderer just stood there in the wind, drenched and blinking, saying doggedly, "Where thou goest I will go." So at last I told him to come on if he must, and gave him a piece of the bread I had in my pocket; then we struggled on together, and thus began the most memorable of all my wild days.

The level flood, driving hard in our faces, thrashed and washed us wildly until we got into the shelter of a grove on the east side of the glacier near the front, where we stopped awhile for breath and to listen and look out. The exploration of the glacier was my main object, but the wind was too high to allow excursions over its open surface, where one might be dangerously shoved while balancing for a jump on the brink of a crevasse. In the meantime the storm was a fine study. Here the end of the glacier, descending an abrupt swell of resisting rock about 500-feet high, leans forward and falls in ice cascades. And as the storm came down the glacier from the north, Stickeen and I were beneath the main current of the blast, while favorably located to see and hear it. What a psalm the storm was singing, and how fresh the smell of the washed earth and leaves, and how sweet the still small voices of the storm! Detached wafts and swirls were coming through the woods, with music from the leaves and branches and furrowed boles, and even from the splintered rocks and ice-crags overhead, many of the tones soft and low and flute-like, as if each leaf and tree, crag and spire were a tuned reed. A broad torrent, draining the side of the glacier, now swollen by scores of new streams from the mountains, was rolling boulders along its rocky channel, with thudding, bumping, muffled sounds, rushing toward the bay with tremendous energy, as if in haste to get out of the mountains; the waters above and beneath calling to each other, and all to the ocean, their home.

Looking southward from our shelter, we had this great torrent and the forested mountain wall above it on our left, the spiry ice-crags on our right, and smooth gray gloom ahead. I tried to draw the marvelous scene in my notebook, but the rain blurred the page in spite of all my pains to shelter it, and the sketch was almost worthless. When the wind began to abate, I traced the east side of the glacier. All the trees standing on the edge of the woods were barked and bruised, showing high-ice mark in a very telling way, while tens of thousands of those that had stood for centuries on the bank of the glacier farther out lay crushed and being crushed. In many places I could see down 50 feet or so beneath the margin of the glacier-mill, where trunks from one to two feet in diameter were being ground to pulp against outstanding rock-ribs and bosses of the bank.

About three miles above the front of the glacier I climbed to the surface of it by means of axe-steps made easy for Stickeen. As far as the eye could reach, the level, or nearly level, glacier stretched away indefinitely beneath the gray sky, a seemingly boundless prairie of ice. The rain continued, and grew colder, which I did not mind, but a dim snowy look in the drooping clouds made me hesitate about venturing far from land. No trace of the west shore was visible, and in case the clouds should settle and give snow, or the wind again become violent, I feared getting caught in a tangle of crevasses. Snow-crystals, the flowers of the mountain clouds, are frail, beautiful things, but terrible when flying on storm-winds in darkening, benumbing swarms or when welded together into glaciers full of deadly crevasses. Watching the weather, I sauntered about on the crystal sea. For a mile or two out I found the ice remarkably safe. The marginal crevasses were mostly narrow, while the few wider ones were easily avoided bypassing around them, and the clouds began to open here and there.

Thus encouraged, I at last pushed out for the other side; for Nature can make us do anything she likes. At first we made rapid progress, and the sky was not very threatening, while I took bearings occasionally with a pocket compass to enable me to find my way back more surely in case the storm should become blinding; but the structure lines of the glacier were my main guide. Toward the west side we came to a closely crevassed section in which we had to make long, narrow tacks and doublings, tracing the edges of tremendous transverse and longitudinal crevasses, many of which were from 20 to 30 feet wide, and perhaps a thousand feet deep—beautiful and awful. In working away through them I was severely cautious, but Stickeen came on as unhesitating as the flying clouds. The widest crevasse that I could jump he would leap without so much as halting to take a look at it. The weather was now making quick changes, scattering bits of dazzling brightness through the wintry gloom; at rare intervals, when the sun broke forth wholly free, the glacier was seen from shore to shore with a bright array of encompassing mountains partly revealed, wearing the clouds as garments, while the prairie bloomed and sparkled with irised light from myriads of washed crystals. Then suddenly all the glorious show would be darkened and blotted out.

Stickeen seemed to care for none of these things, bright or dark, nor for the crevasses, wells, moulins, or swift flashing streams into which he might fall. The little adventurer was only about two years old, yet nothing seemed novel to him, nothing daunted him. He showed neither caution nor curiosity, wonder nor fear, but bravely trotted on as if glaciers were playgrounds. His stout, muffled body seemed all one skipping muscle, and it was truly wonderful to see how swiftly and to all appearance heedlessly he flashed across nerve-trying chasms six or eight feet wide. His courage was so unwavering that it seemed to be due to dullness of perception, as if he were only blindly bold; and I kept warning him to be careful. For we had been close companions on so many wilderness trips that I had formed the habit of talking to him as if he were a boy and understood every word.

We gained the west shore in about three hours; the width of the glacier here being about seven miles. Then I pushed northward in order to see as far back as possible into the fountains of the Fairweather Mountains, in case the clouds should rise. The walking was easy along the margin of the forest, which, of course, like that on the other side, had been invaded and crushed by the swollen, overflowing glacier. In an hour or so, after passing a massive headland, we came suddenly on a branch of the glacier, which, in the form of a magnificent ice-cascade two miles wide, was pouring over the rim of the main basin in a westerly direction, its surface broken into wave-shaped blades and shattered blocks, suggesting the wildest updashing, heaving, plunging motion of a great river cataract. Tracing it down three or four miles, I found that it discharged into a lake, filling it with icebergs.

I would gladly have followed the lake outlet to tide-water, but the day was already far spent, and the threatening sky called for haste on the return trip to get off the ice before dark. I decided therefore to go no farther, and, after taking a general view of the wonderful region, turned back, hoping to see it again under more favorable auspices. We made good speed up the canon of the great ice-torrent, and out on the main glacier until we had left the west shore about two miles behind us. Here we got into a difficult network of crevasses, the gathering clouds began to drop misty fringes, and soon the dreaded snow came flying thick and fast. I now began to feel anxious about finding a way in the blurring storm, Stickeen showed no trace of fear. He was still the same silent, able little hero. I noticed, however, that after the storm-darkness came on he kept close up behind me. The snow urged us to make still greater haste, but at the same time hid our way. I pushed on as best I could, jumping innumerable crevasses, and for every hundred rods or so of direct advance traveling a mile in doubling up and down in the turmoil of chasms and dislocated ice-blocks. After an hour or two of this work we came to a series of longitudinal crevasses of appalling width, and almost straight and regular in trend, like immense furrows. These I traced with firm nerve, excited and strengthened by the danger, making wide jumps, poising cautiously on their dizzy edges after cutting hallows for my feet before making the spring, to avoid possible slipping or any uncertainty on the farther sides, where only one trial is granted—exercise at once frightful and inspiring. Stickeen followed seemingly without effort.

Many a mile we thus traveled, mostly up and down, making but little real headway in crossing, running instead of walking most of the time as the danger of being compelled to spend the night on the glacier became threatening. Stickeen seemed able for anything. Doubtless we could have weathered the storm for one night, dancing on a flat spot to keep from freezing, and I faced the threat without feeling anything like despair; but we were hungry and wet, and the wind from the mountains was still thick with snow and bitterly cold, so of course that night would have seemed a very long one. I could not see far enough through the blurring snow to judge in which general direction the least dangerous route lay, while the few dim, momentary glimpses I caught of mountains through rifts in the flying clouds were far from encouraging either as weather signs or as guides. I had simply to grope my way from crevasse to crevasse, holding a general direction by the ice-structure, which was not to be seen every-where, and partly by the wind. Again and again I was put to my mettle, but Stickeen followed easily, his nerve apparently growing more unflinch-ing as the danger increased. So it always is with mountaineers when hard beset. Running hard and jumping, holding every minute of the remain-ing daylight, poor as it was, precious, we doggedly persevered and tried to hope that every difficult crevasse we overcame would prove to be the last of its kind. But on the contrary, as we advanced they became more deadly trying.

At length our way was barred by a very wide and straight crevasse, which I traced rapidly northward a mile or so without finding a crossing or hope of one; then down the glacier about as far, to where it united with another uncrossable crevasse. In all this distance of perhaps two miles there was only one place where I could possibly jump it, but the width of this jump was the utmost I dared attempt, while the danger of slipping on the farther side was so great that I was loath to try it. Furthermore, the side I was on was about a foot higher than the other, and even with this advantage the crevasse seemed dangerously wide. One is liable to un-derestimate the width of crevasses where the magnitudes in general are great. I therefore stared at this one mighty keenly, estimating its width and the shape of the edge on the farther side, until I thought that I could jump it if necessary, but that in case I should be compelled to jump back from the lower side I might fail. Now, a cautious mountaineer seldom takes a step on unknown ground which seems at all dangerous that be cannot retrace in case he should be stopped by unseen obstacles ahead. This is the rule of mountaineers who live long, and, though in haste, I compelled myself to sit down and calmly deliberate before I broke it.

Retracing my devious path in imagination as if it were drawn on a chart, I saw that I was recrossing the glacier a mile or two farther upstream than the course pursued in the morning, and that I was now entangled in a section I had not before seen. Should I risk this dangerous jump, or try to regain the woods on the west shore, make a fire, and have only hunger to endure while waiting for a new day? I had already crossed so broad a stretch of dangerous ice that I saw it would be difficult to get back to the woods through the storm, before dark, and the attempt would most likely result in a dismal nightdance on the glacier; while just beyond the present barrier the surface seemed more promising, and the east shore was now perhaps about as near as the west. I was therefore eager to go on. But this wide jump was a dreadful obstacle.

At length, because of the dangers already behind me, I determined to venture against those that might be ahead, jumped and landed well, but with so little to spare that I more than ever dreaded being compelled to take that jump back from the lower side. Stickeen followed, making nothing of it, and we ran eagerly forward, hoping we were leaving all our troubles behind. But within the distance of a few hundred yards we were stopped by the widest crevasse yet encountered. Of course I made haste to explore it, hoping all might yet be remedied by finding a bridge or a way around either end. About three-fourths of a mile upstream I found that it united with the one we had just crossed, as I feared it would. Then, tracing it down, I found it joined the same crevasse at the lower end also, maintaining throughout its whole course a width of 40 to 50 feet. Thus to my dismay I discovered that we were on a narrow island about two miles long, with two barely possible ways of escape: one back by the way we came, the other ahead by an almost inaccessible sliver-bridge that crossed the great crevasse from near the middle of it!

After this nerve-trying discovery I ran back to the sliver-bridge and cautiously examined it. Crevasses, caused by strains from variations in the rate of motion of different parts of the glacier and convexities in the channel, are mere cracks when they first open, so narrow as hardly to admit the blade of a pocket-knife, and gradually widen according to the extent of the strain and the depth of the glacier. Now some of these cracks are interrupted, like the cracks in wood, and in opening, the strip of ice between overlapping ends is dragged out, and may maintain a continuous connection between the sides, just as the two sides of a slivered crack in wood that is being split are connected. Some crevasses remain open for months or even years, and by the melting of their sides continue to increase in width long after the opening strain has ceased; while the sliver-bridges, level on top at first and perfectly safe, are at length melted to thin, vertical, knife-edged blades, the upper portion being most exposed to the weather; and since the exposure is greatest in the middle, they at length curve downward like the cables of suspension bridges. This one was evidently very old, for it had been weathered and wasted until it was the most dangerous and inaccessible that ever lay in my way. The width of the crevasse was here about 50 feet, and the sliver crossing diagonally was about 70 feet long; its thin knife-edge near the middle was depressed 25 or 30 feet below the level of the glacier, and the upcurving ends were attached to the sides eight or ten feet below the brink. Getting down the nearly vertical wall to the end of the sliver and up the other side were the main difficulties, and they seemed all but insurmountable. Of the many perils encountered in my years of wandering on mountains and glaciers none seemed so plain and stern and merciless as this. And it was presented when we were wet to the skin and hungry, the sky dark with quick driving snow, and the night near. But we were forced to face it. It was a tremendous necessity.

Beginning, not immediately above the sunken end of the bridge, but a little to one side, I cut a deep hollow on the brink for my knees to rest in. Then, leaning over, with my shorthandled axe I cut a step 16 or 18 inches below, which on account of the sheerness of the wall was necessarily shallow. That step, however, was well made; its floor sloped slightly inward and formed a good hold for my heels. Then, slipping cautiously upon it, and crouching as low as possible, with my left side toward the wall, I steadied myself against the wind with my left hand in a slight notch, while with the right I cut other similar steps and notches in succession, guarding against losing balance by glinting of the axe, or by wind-gusts, for life and death were in every stroke and in the niceness of finish of every foothold.

After the end of the bridge was reached I chipped it down until I had made a level platform six or eight inches wide, and it was a trying thing to poise on this little slippery platform while bending over to get safely astride of the sliver. Crossing was then comparatively easy by chipping off the sharp edge with short, careful strokes, and hitching forward an inch or two at a time, keeping my balance with my knees pressed against the sides, the tremendous abyss on either hand studiously ignored. To me the edge of that blue sliver was then all the world. But the most trying part of the adventure, after working my way across inch by inch and chipping another small platform, was to rise from the safe position astride and to cut a step-ladder in the nearly vertical face of the wall—chipping, climbing, holding on with feet and fingers in mere notches. At such times one's whole body is eye, and common skill and fortitude are replaced by power beyond our call or knowledge. Never before had I been so long under deadly strain. How I got up that cliff I never could tell. The thing seemed to have been done by somebody else. I never have held death in contempt, though in the course of my explorations I have oftentimes felt that to meet one's fate on a noble mountain, or in the heart of a glacier, would be blessed as compared with death from disease, or from some shabby lowland accident. But the best death, quick and crystal-pure, set so glaringly open before us, is hard enough to face, even though we feel gratefully sure that we have already had happiness enough for a dozen lives.

But poor Stickeen, the wee, hairy, sleek beastie, think of him! When I had decided to dare the bridge, and while I was on my knees chipping a hollow on the rounded brow above it, he came behind me, pushed his head past my shoulder, looked down and across, scanned the sliver and its approaches with his mysterious eyes, then looked me in the face with a startled air of surprise and concern, and began to mutter and whine; saying as plainly as if speaking with words, "Surely, you are not going into that awful place." This was the first time I had seen him gaze deliberately into a crevasse, or into my face with an eager, speaking, troubled look. That he should have recognized and appreciated the danger at the first glance showed wonderful sagacity. Never before had the daring midget seemed to know that ice was slippery or that there was any such thing as danger anywhere. His looks and tones of voice when he began to complain and speak his fears were so human that I unconsciously talked to him in sympathy as I would to a frightened boy, and in trying to calm his fears perhaps in some measure moderated my own. "Hush your fears, my boy," I said, "we will get across safe, though it is not going to be easy. No right way is easy in this rough world. We must risk our lives to save them. At the worst we can only slip, and then how grand a grave we will have, and by and by our nice bones will do good in the terminal moraine."

But my sermon was far from reassuring him: he began to cry, and after taking another piercing look at the tremendous gulf, ran away in desperate excitement, seeking some other crossing. By the time he got back, baffled of course, I had made a step or two. I dared not look back, but he made himself heard; and when he saw that I was certainly bent on crossing he cried aloud in despair. The danger was enough to daunt anybody, but it seems wonderful that he should have been able to weigh and appreciate it so justly. No mountaineer could have seen it more quickly or judged it more wisely, discriminating between real and apparent peril.

When I gained the other side, he screamed louder than ever, and after running back and forth in vain search for a way of escape, he would return to the brink of the crevasse above the bridge, moaning and wailing as if in the bitterness of death. Could this be the silent, philosophic Stickeen? I shouted encouragement, telling him the bridge was not so bad as it looked, that I had left it flat and safe for his feet, and he could walk it easily. But he was afraid to try. Strange so small an animal should be capable of such big, wise fears. I called again and again in a reassuring tone to come on and fear nothing; that he could come if he would only try. He would hush for a moment, look down again at the bridge, and shout his unshakable conviction that he could never, never come that way; then lie back in despair, as if howling, "O-o-oh! What a place! No-o-o, I can never go-o-o down there!" His natural composure and courage had vanished utterly in a tumultuous storm of fear. Had the danger been less, his distress would have seemed ridiculous. But in this dismal, merciless abyss lay the shadow of death, and his heartrending cries might well have called Heaven to his help. Perhaps they did. So bidden before, he was now transparent, and one could see the workings of his heart and mind like the movements of a clock out of its case. His voice and gestures, hopes and fears, were so perfectly human that none could mistake them; while he seemed to understand every word of mine. I was troubled at the thought of having to leave him out all night, and of the danger of not finding him in the morning. It seemed impossible to get him to venture. To compel him to try through fear of being abandoned, I started off as if leaving him to his fate, and disappeared back of a hummock; but this did no good; he only lay down and moaned in utter hopeless misery. So, after hiding a few minutes, I went back to the brink of the crevasse and in a severe tone of voice shouted across to him that now I must certainly leave him, I could wait no longer, and that, if he would not come, all I could promise was that I would return to seek him next day. I warned him that if he went back to the woods the wolves would kill him, and finished by urging him once more by words and gestures to come on, come on. He knew very well what I meant, and at last, with the courage of despair, hushed and breathless, he crouched down on the brink in the hollow I had made for my knees, pressed his body against the ice as if trying to get the advantage of the friction of every hair, gazed into the first step, put his little feet together and slid them slowly, slowly over the edge and down into it, bunching all four in it and almost standing on his head. Then, without lifting his feet, as well as I could see through the snow, he slowly worked them over the edge of the step and down into the next and the next in succession in the same way, and gained the end of the bridge. Then, lifting his feet with the regularity and slowness of the vibrations of a seconds pendulum, as if counting and measuring *one-two-three*, holding himself steady against the gusty wind, and giving separate attention to each little step, he gained the foot of the cliff, while I was on my knees leaning over to give him a lift should he succeed in getting within reach of my arm. Here he halted in dead silence, and it was here I feared he might fail, for dogs are poor climbers. I had no cord. If I had had one, I would have dropped a noose over his head and hauled him up. But while I was thinking whether an available cord might be made out of clothing, he was looking keenly into the series of notched steps and finger-holds I had made, as if counting them, and fixing the position of each one of them in his mind. Then suddenly up he came in a springy rush, hooking his paws into the steps and notches so quickly that I could not see how it was done, and whizzed past my head, safe at last!

And now came a scene! "Well done, well done, little boy! Brave boy!" I cried, trying to catch and caress him; but he would not be caught. Never before or since have I seen anything like so passionate a revulsion from the depths of despair to exultant, triumphant, uncontrollable joy. He flashed and darted hither and thither as if fairly demented, screaming and shouting, swirling round and round in giddy loops and circles like a leaf in a whirlwind, lying down, and rolling over and over, sidewise and heels over head, and pouring forth a tumultuous flood of hysterical cries and sobs and gasping mutterings. When I ran up to him to shake him, fearing he might die of joy, he flashed off two or three hundred yards, his feet in a mist of motion; then, turning suddenly, came back in a wild rush and launched himself at my face, almost knocking me down, all the time screeching and screaming and shouting as if saying, "Saved! saved! saved!" Then away again, dropping suddenly at times with his feet in the air, trembling and fairly sobbing. Such passionate emotion was enough to kill him. Moses' stately song of triumph after escaping the Egyptians and the Red Sea was nothing to it. Who could have guessed the capacity of the dull, enduring little fellow for all that most stirs this mortal frame? Nobody could have helped crying with him!

But there is nothing like work for toning down excessive fear or joy. So I ran ahead, calling him in as gruff a voice as I could command to come on and stop his nonsense, for we had far to go and it would soon be dark. Neither of us feared another trial like this. Heaven would surely count one enough for a lifetime. The ice ahead was gashed by thousands of crevasses, but they were common ones. The joy of deliverance burned in us like fire, and we ran without fatigue, every muscle with immense rebound glorying in its strength. Stickeen flew across everything in his way, and not till dark did he settle into his normal fox-like trot. At last the cloudy mountains came in sight, and we soon felt the solid rock beneath our feet, and were safe.

Then came weakness. Danger had vanished, and so had our strength. We tottered down the lateral moraine in the dark, over boulders and tree trunks, through the bushes and devil-club thickets of the grove where we had sheltered ourselves in the morning, and across the level mud-slope of the terminal moraine. We reached camp about ten o'clock, and found a big fire and a big supper. A party of Hoona Indians had visited Mr. Young, bringing a gift of porpoise meat and wild strawberries, and Hunter Joe had brought in a wild goat. But we lay down, too tired to eat much, and soon fell into a troubled sleep. The man who said, "The harder the toil, the sweeter the rest," never was profoundly tired. Stickeen kept springing up and muttering in his sleep, no doubt dreaming that he was still on the brink of the crevasse; and so did I, that night and many others long afterward, when I was overtired.

Thereafter Stickeen was a changed dog. During the rest of the trip, instead of holding aloof, he always lay by my side, tried to keep me constantly in sight, and would hardly accept a morsel of food, however tempting, from any hand but mine. At night, when all was quiet about the campfire, he would come to me and rest his head on my knee with a look of devotion as if I were his god. And often as he caught my eye he seemed to be trying to say, "Wasn't that an awful time we had together on the glacier?"

Nothing in after years has dimmed that Alaska storm-day. As I write it all comes rushing and roaring to mind as if I were again in the heart of it. Again I see the gray flying clouds with their rain-floods and snow, the ice-cliffs towering above the shrinking forest, the majestic ice cascade, the vast glacier outspread before its white mountain fountains, and in the heart of it the tremendous crevasse—emblem of the valley of the shadow of death—low clouds trailing over it, the snow falling into it; and on its brink I see little Stickeen, and I hear his cries for help and his shouts of joy. I have known many dogs, and many a story I could tell of their wisdom and devotion; but to none do I owe so much as to Stickeen. At first the least promising and least known of my dog-friends, he suddenly became the best known of them all. Our storm-battle for life brought him to light, and through him as through a window I have ever since been looking with deeper sympathy into all my fellow mortals.

None of Stickeen's friends knows what finally became of him. After my work for the season was done I departed for California, and I never saw the dear little fellow again. In reply to anxious inquiries his master wrote me that in the summer of 1883 he was stolen by a tourist at Fort Wrangel and taken away on a steamer. His fate is wrapped in mystery. Doubtless he has left this world—crossed the last crevasse—and gone to another. But he will not be forgotten. To me Stickeen is immortal.

SUMMER AND WINTER ASCENTS

by Dennis Schmitt

*T*he richly hyped solo climbs of "hero" mountaineers can obscure the fact that soloing is an intensely personal affair that can produce other things besides historical achievements and controversies. *At all levels of difficulty, soloing is a meditation of sorts. In the following essay, Dennis Schmitt recounts several unremarkable solo ascents of several nameless mountains in Alaska. Few would ever remember what Schmitt did, and fewer still would care. And yet in the heart of these seemingly ordinary technical achievements, Schmitt found a quiet, graceful depth of experience normally lost on climbers committed to do-or-die climbs.*

‡   ‡   ‡

On and off and on I have been somewhat of a mountaineer in the Brooks Range for ten years now since I was 19. Yet even as a child I had dreams of a range of mountains somewhere so far north that the Big Dipper and the North Star stood above them at the zenith of the sky, a mountain range that formed a magical ring around the North Pole and protected Santa Claus from such pedestrian influences as the Fourth of July. When I first saw a map of the Brooks Range in my later childhood I immediately took them to be these same mountains. Moreover I took them to be a concretely logical extension of the hills in my backyard making their way north along the Pacific border of the American continent. You may be sure that by the time I had at last arrived in Anaktuvuk Pass, a Nunamiut Inuit (Eskimo) village in the middle of the Brooks Range in 1965, I had already dreamed my way into their fabled midst many times over. And I can say,

without reservation, that the age-old dreamer within me was vindi-
cated by what he saw—a landscape for which I felt an instant nostalgia,
a landscape that inspired deep within me a terrible longing never to
die, never to go blind to the world, a landscape of beautiful people
magically different from myself, as true a fairy tale as ever I have wit-
nessed on earth.

All through the late summer, fall and early winter of that year I focused my energies toward adapting to Nunamiut village life, learning to
handle the dog teams, to kill, skin, and prepare meat, to gather willow
fuel, to speak the language, to mend my Tannik (white man's) personality
and to look only passively around at the horizon, inhibiting any mountaineering ambitions I might have. Then late in February, when life was
very difficult, the men and dogs having left the village in a desperate
search for caribou, and the women and children having merged house-
holds to consolidate body heat and conserve fuel, I suddenly felt the urge
to escape from village life into the world of the pyramids and pinnacles
above me.

Three miles north of the village was Peak 5,280, gleaming in the noon
twilight. "Things couldn't be much worse up there," I thought. "At least
there's a little sunlight in the middle of the day." Perhaps too I thought of
impressing the locals with my spirit of adventure in the already brutal
face of things. Hearing of my plans for an ascent they, however, assured
me that whatever the outcome they would not be impressed whatsoever.
In the blowing snow, mist and darkness of that same afternoon I was
pulling a sled-load of ice with an older Nunamiut man near the grave-
yard north of the village. He warned me that if I should die on the
mountain I would be buried as unmomentously and cheaply as possible
and be entirely forgotten by spring. He showed me how hard the frozen
ground was to dig. Pointing out a possible plot for myself, only half in
jest, I told him that I would nevertheless be careful. He thanked me,
though I knew how dearly he would, in truth, enjoy seeing a Tannik dead.
He was the sort of man who saw human mortality as an opportunity for
revenge against his enemies rather than as a threat to himself. He loved
to play with the vocabulary of death, both in English and Eskimo, and
continued in that manner, despite the dark and wind, all the way back to
the village.

The equipment by which I would either live or die on this ascent was
Paleolithic. I had brought some fine caribou calf skins from hunting in
the eastern mountains while living in a Kutchin village the summer before. Two beautiful Nunamiut girls and their observant mothers helped

me prepare these skins and cut and sew them into a parka and pants. An older, more occasionally divine lady made me some caribou-skin boots for a good price, and another lady with as sweet a soul as God ever conceived, completed my outfit with inner socks and mittens. She was shedding tears for me as I put on my satchel and makeshift, soft-bound skis to set out for the base of Peak 5,280. This peak is called Suakpuk (big scold) by the Nunamiut (the Geological Survey map designates Peak 5,883, four miles to the west, as Suakpuk. Such discrepancies are entirely usual in much of Alaska). It is a startlingly dramatic peak and is composed of great walled layers of nearly horizontal limestone, which constitute the predominating formation in this part of the range. Its southern buttress, an exquisite limestone pyramid, dominates the village as a cathedral dominates a medieval European city. North of the pyramid lie two steeply ridged gullies and then the imposing vertical limestone walls of the northeastern face. The summit is a series of pinnacles, the southernmost being the highest.

High at the base of the south gully I left my skis and discovered that my wolf-dog, Shillig, had followed my trail and would soon be upon me. I waited for her as I checked my equipment, which was limited to my clothing, a thermometer, dried meat, cookies, and an old camera. The snow was very dry and I knew I would be thirsty before long. Shillig and I proceeded up the deep snows of the gully, moving toward the right-hand ridge until, at an altitude of less than 4,000 feet, we were climbing up the buttresses and chimneys of the ridge proper. The separate ascents of some of these buttresses involved technical difficulties, although vertical exposures were not more than 40 feet.

I proved to be Shillig's vehicle for much of the route—I climbed with her over my shoulders. Occasionally I had to throw her bodily up a face to ledges where I left her clinging and howling desperately as I made my own way. On one occasion, as she stood on my shoulders, I was on the verge of losing my footing on a wall of conglomerate. "Get up and jump! Jump, Shillig, jump!" I cried as I began to slip. And she did indeed jump as I fell, burking my shoulders and knees and at last crashing against a steep wall of hard snow. I brushed the snow out of my neck and looked up to see her 40 feet above me, gazing down disconsolately and silently. "Well, you got the best of that one," I told her. As we started again, the snow was getting harder, and we were buffeted more and more by the winds of the summit ridge. In the high wind, climbing on the hard-packed snows of the ridge proved very treacherous with my caribou-skin bottoms and I suffered many helpless falls. The summit was reached by traversing an exposed ledge beneath an overhang. From the summit I gazed down on the limestone pyramid forming the south rampart of the mountain and could see the village beyond and far below. "So that is where I have been living all this time," I said to myself. "I would never really have known where it was otherwise." The village itself appeared as an inadvertent exception to the Arctic nothingness that engulfed it. I imagined how pitiful I might appear to a god or a spaceman (or even an airline pilot, for that matter) looking down from a little higher still.

It was minus 29 degrees Fahrenheit and as the wind was continuing to rise, I could not long contemplate the landscape. I left in twilight and high winds, working my way into the protected hollows of the eastern face. Even in descending, I had to be very careful to avoid any exertion that might frost my lungs. On a milder note, however, there was surprisingly little risk of avalanche due to the dry winter climate of this region and I was able to use avalanche chutes in making my descent. At the base of the mountain the weather had turned extremely cold and a strong north wind almost literally blew me back into the village. There I drank my tea, ate my food and graciously let myself be reacquainted with the warm bathtub of village life.

South of the village lies an eloquent valley called Inukpuk or Great Spirit. It is dominated by a pyramid, Peak 4,850, with a steep, fluted north face. This valley and peak had intrigued my mountaineering sensibilities for some time, and one afternoon as I was scraping sheep skins and looking out the window at the peak, I received another warning. The Nunamiut lady who had made my mittens told me darkly, "No one ever went *that* way (up that mountain) . . . you really shouldn't go away that way again." She did not speak English and I had always felt that accounted in some measure for the exquisite gentility of her nature. I told her that I had terrible doubts about the mountain myself, but that I might go anyway just to spite myself. The next morning I told her to look for sunlight on the summit not long after noon. I left the village, alone in darkness with a north wind at my back and the temperature at minus 28 degrees, carrying in my satchel leather climbing boots, food, water, a camera and a mirror. I reached the base of the north face directly under the summit. From here the face appeared much steeper and longer than it had earlier. I was apprehensive and exhilarated as I began to climb, sensing my whole life flickering about me in all its transient detail. I made my way up the very steep ridge to the left of the chute leading to the obvious notch east of the summit. From an altitude of 3,000 feet I was forced to climb difficult fourth-class chimneys and a few very exposed buttresses. I found myself all but trapped at many junctures. The ascent would not have been possible without climbing boots and was not reasonable without ropes. The latter fact made for a richly emotional climb. As many times as I found myself cramped against the edge of oblivion, I found myself also falling in love with some new female from out of my past. On the summit, after tunneling through a cornice, I forgot all this and settled back into my skin boots to warm my frozen feet. I found a cairn there and a note of previous ascent by Steven Porter, a geologist, on "July first, 1959, via the east ridge in hail and snow." So my Nunamiut friend had been mistaken; someone else had been up here.

The temperature on the summit was minus 31 degrees. I took out my mirror and reflected a glimmer of the low afternoon sunlight into the village, verifying both my success and survival. Just then, in a misty temperature inversion over Inukpuk Valley, I thought I saw the face of a laughing man out of the corner of my eye. Yet when I looked at it straight on it was gone.

The descent down the steep, very hard windblown snow of the west ridge was very treacherous. To return to the village I had to battle my way north along the bare ice of the river against 40- to 60-mile winds. The ground visibility was totally obscured by blowing snow, and yet above me great waves of aurora loomed throughout the black sky between the mountain walls. As blinded as I was, I felt utterly blessed in that I was nevertheless not utterly blind.

In the spring that followed these first winter ascents I began to move freely about the landscape, traveling by whim for days at a time with only such food as I could catch along the way. My mountaineering even proved useful to the Nunamiut when I was able to climb into the clouds, find the caribou and coax them down into ambush on group hunting expeditions. Roaming about in the fogs of the upper slopes I acquainted myself, furthermore, with every form of mammal known to that region. I ignored, however, the summits. For the time being I felt I had learned whatever they had to teach.

A few years later I was berry picking with some Nunamiut women and children in Inukpuk Valley under the north face of Peak 4,850 when one lady pointed the mountain out to me. "You hear what someone says," she smiled, "someone says *that* mountain is Dennis Mountain. Ekkayoak (my Eskimo name) Mountain! You . . ."

I saw the pyramid reflected in her eyes and realized finally what she had said. "My mountain," I said tentatively. "My mountain!" I cried with greater assurance, gazing blankly into space with a feeling the pharaohs must have felt. "Ekkayoak, Ekkayoak Mountain is better than Dennis Mountain," I said matter-of-factly. "It's all temporary, of course, but still Ekkayoak is much, much better than Dennis as a name for a mountain."

The lady suddenly broke out into laughter—wild, playful laughter. "I jokes," she said, "I jokes you real good on that time. You think someone can *give* you the mountain? No, no . . . even Nunamiut can't do that." At that I paused, reflected and collapsed in dismay. And so it was that Peak 4,850, as if in a comedian's dream, brought me within a breath of immortality but did not let me stick. Of course, nowadays who knows whose mountain it is. I truly believe I was up there once, but it's getting harder and harder to remember.

THE ABATTOIR

by Mark Twight

*T*o the solo climber, the route to the top is strewn with land mines—
yet the soloist forges higher and higher because once committed,
the only way off is straight up. Somewhere en route, a scream will
break the silence—a scream with no sound but with a clear message. Up
from the long years and the long tensions bursts that strange, clarified
moment when the soloist knows that the next move might be his last.
Perhaps it's the curious virtue of this moment that so enchants the soloist,
and by proxy, the risk-taker in all of us who devour these accounts. In
the following story, a solo ice climber, filled with the presence of himself,
feels the gravity of what bullfighters call "The Moment of Truth."

‡   ‡   ‡

It was an hour before I could move my legs. The rock hit so hard I thought
it broke my spine. Tears burst from my eyes with the impact. I saw every
dream and hope vanish with the rock. I began to fall. I said bitter, acid
good-byes in my head, convinced my life would end splattered obscenely
across the talus. The black thoughts pulled up short as I came onto the
wrist leash of my ice tool. It stopped the plunge. My shoulder didn't separate but I could tell it was bad.

For a moment I felt elated. I'd saved myself. I retained control of the
situation. Seconds later the blood drained out of my head. My face was the
color of concrete—the color of a corpse. I was in trouble: thousands of feet
up in the winter quiet, all alone on 80-degree ice and apoplectic. The pain
arrested my breath. Snow fell from the gray sky. The wind lectured me

about the futility of my future; I heard the primitive voice of the masses saying that I could not succeed. I was becoming another child prodigy whose life is apprehended by circumstance. I didn't want to die . . .

I climbed up this north face to experience the masochistic pleasure of fighting for my life. But I hadn't intended to lose. The need for risk has always been inside of me, lurking and threatening. If I don't satisfy the impulses, if I let them build up untreated, they'll explode with finality. I'd kill myself trying to handle it.

I wondered how long the pick might hold with all of my weight on it. I'd given my precious ice tools more attention than I gave most of my friends. I felt guilty when the picks rusted or remained blunt after some epic drove me out of the mountains. I could feel the tools despise me when I ignored them. I despised them too for allowing me to fulfill my obsession. Often I threw them into the basement as punishment for letting me get in too deep. On days like today though I praised them for their greatness. I loved them for being good enough to push me this hard. When the rock hit me I dropped my favorite hammer, a grievous loss but not as awful as seeing my spare firmly placed above me—out of reach.

The missile was huge, the size of a milk crate I think. But I didn't hear any of my bones break. I tried moving immediately after the concussive blow and my legs jerked uselessly. They felt like a fish's tail, waving back and forth in front of the blood-dyed-terra-cotta ice. A ten-inch rent gaped in my Goretex suit and as the stain dried, the fabric stuck to my skin. I couldn't see the bruise swelling on the back of my thigh.

More rocks winged by with the shriek of living things. The air was warming up and the ice began to flow with water. Fear washed over me in rivulets, then torrents. My right hand groped for something solid to pull up on and my forearms cramped until they too were paralyzed. No experience or training had prepared me for the anxious torment of dying slowly—and knowing it. I always thought it would come as quick as a bullet. I could never face the creeping certainty of a terminal illness. As it was, my bloodshot eyes were overwhelmed by tears and I started groaning. I was giving up on life surely, willfully—and the tape hadn't ended yet. I'd chosen the blackest music for this route—it would have been the hardest climb I'd ever done.

We burned and burned, I was a cinder body and soul . . . comfort is treachery so pound nails in tight eyes screaming out of sight against a grain like curtain — unbearably alive.

Skinny Puppy

Mark Twight, called Dr. Doom by some because of his dark writing style, has carved a unique niche for himself in the annals of alpine climbing. PHOTO: TWIGHT COLLECTION

"Alive?" I thought, "until today I was hardly alive at all. But I'm too much so now, and I want more." I used to be afraid that I would die young but after living for awhile I got scared that I wouldn't.

My toes burned. My leg and hip were shot through with pain. What a sensation; life returned to deadened limbs. I wiggled my toes one by one. I fought to move the whole leg. I chased down and tackled the hope I had given up. Something screamed inside, telling me it was time to fight back, not give in. It reminded me of the physical therapy after doctors rebuilt my knee. I remember trying as hard as I could to bend my leg and not being able to. The frustration was infinite, quitting so very seductive. Disillusions followed setbacks but I finally bent it. I finally lifted some weights, and this gave me the hope that I might climb again.

The first time I tried to rest weight on my crampons the left leg collapsed. I fell wincing back onto my ice tool, imploring it to save me. My thigh kept swelling; pulsed and stiffened. I tried again. I was determined to stand on it. After I stabilized myself on the crampon's frontpoints, putting as little weight on them as I could, I stared up at the spare tool. It was the key to survival, and it was out of reach. As lactic acid poisoned my contracted biceps they began to jump with the strain.

I couldn't remove the tool in my left hand to place it higher—not without falling off. I tried halfheartedly to lock off on it and grab the tool above.

I could not do it. I worked my feet up the ice inch by agonizing inch. Lightning rods of pain carved through the meat of my legs every time I flexed them. I drew closer. Breath heaved out of my lungs. I coughed and it felt like something tearing. I roared with frustration, enraged with my own weakness. In a rally of effort I muscled up, ignoring the cramps—and lunged for the ice tool's wristleash. But all I saw was the other tool, the one that held me, ripping out of the ice. The following seconds wound by brutally, taking their own sweet time.

The adze chopped into the bridge of my nose and blood splattered across the ice. I fell away from it, knocked backwards by the impact. I did one back-flip before my crampons caught a rock—shattering my ankle—and catapulted me out over the soulless, battered slope. I plunged into the end. Music wailed through my headphones. What was once "the last ride" mused about in barrooms became the real and horrifying truth. I knew I wouldn't hit anything on the way down, just the talus that was lightly dusted with snow.

CLIMBING GLOSSARY

aid: using means other than the action of hands, feet, and body to get up a climb

abseil: to rappel

anchor: a means by which climbers are secured to a cliff

arete: an outside corner of rock

armbar, armlock: a means of holding onto a wide crack

bashie: a piece of malleable metal that's been hammered into a rock seam as an anchor: used in extreme aid climbing

belay: procedure of securing a climber by the use of rope

beta: detailed route information, sometimes move by move

No, this photo's not turned sideways—incredibly, Wolfgang Gullich is soloing Separate Reality, *a 5.12 roof crack hundreds of feet off the deck in Yosemite Valley.*
PHOTO BY HEINZ ZAK

bergschrund: gap where a glacier meets rock

bight: a loop (as in a bight of rope)

biners: see carabiners

bollard: a naturally constructed ice and snow anchor

bolt: an artificial anchor placed in a hole drilled for that purpose

bomber or bombproof: absolutely fail-safe (as in a very solid anchor or combination of anchors)

bucket: a handhold large enough to fully latch onto, like the handle of a bucket

cam: to lodge in a crack by counterpressure: that which lodges

carabiners: aluminum alloy rings equipped with a spring- loaded snap gate; sometimes called biners and crabs

ceiling: an overhang of sufficient size to loom overhead

chimney (n): a wide fissure in a rock wall, similar in size to a fireplace

chimney (v): to climb said feature

chock: a wedge or mechanical device that provides an anchor in a rock crack

chockstone: a rock lodged in a crack

clean: a description of routes that may be variously free of vegetation, loose rock or the need to place pitons; also the act of removing chocks from a pitch

coldshut: a relatively soft metal ring that can be closed with a hammer blow; notoriously unreliable for withstanding high loads

crabs: carabiners

crampon: metal spikes that attach to climbing boots and provide traction on ice and snow

crimper: a small but positive edge

crux: the most difficult section of a climb or pitch

dihedral: an inside corner of rock

drag: usually used in reference to the resistance of rope through carabiners

Dulfersitz: a method of rappelling that involves wrapping the rope around the body and using the resulting friction

dynamic or dyno: lunge move

edge: a small rock ledge, or the act of standing on an edge

exposure: that relative situation where a climb has particularly noticeable sheerness

face climbing: climbing features on a rock face that does not have cracks

fifi: an un-gated hook used to quickly attach a climber to an anchor

figure-eight (figure-8): a device used for rappelling and belaying; or, a knot used in climbing

free, free climb, or free ascent: to climb using hands and feet only; the rope is only used to safeguard against injury, not for upward progress or resting

French technique: a method of ascending and descending low angle ice and snow with crampons

glissade: to slide down a snowfield on one's rump or feet

goldline: static climbing ropes of yesteryear

gobis: hand abrasions

hangdog: when a leader hangs from a piece of protection to rest, then continues on without lowering back to the ground; not a free ascent

jam: wedging feet, hands, fingers or other body parts to gain purchase in a crack

jugs: like a jug handle

lead: to be first on a climb, placing protection with which to protect oneself

lieback: the climbing maneuver that entails pulling with the hands while pushing with the feet

line: the path of weakness in the rock which is the route

mantle: the climbing maneuver used to gain a single feature above one's head

monodoigts: very small holes or holds, about finger size

move: movement; one of a series of motions necessary to gain climbing distance

nut: same as a chock: a mechanical devise that, by various means, provides a secure anchor to the rock

offwidth: a crack that does not readily accept finger, hand or fist jams

on-sight: to climb a route without prior knowledge or experience of the moves, and without falling or otherwise weighting the rope (also on-sight flash)

opposition: nuts, anchors or climbing maneuvers that are held in place by the simultaneous stress of two forces working against each other

pendulum: to swing on a rope from an anchor to reach an otherwise unreachable feature off to the side

pinkpoint: to lead (without falling) a climb that has been pre-protected with anchors rigged with carabiners

pins: pitons

pitch: the section of rock between belays

pitons: metal spikes of various shapes, hammered into the rock to provide anchors in cracks (also pins or pegs)

placement: the quality of a nut or anchor

protection or pro: the anchors used to safeguard the leader

prusik: both the knot and any means by which one mechanically ascends a rope

quickdraws: short slings with biners that help provide drag-free rope management for the leader

rappel: to descend a rope by means of mechanical brake devices

redpoint: to lead a route, clipping protection as you go, without falling or resting on pro

RP: small nut used mostly in aid climbing

runout: the distance between two points of protection; often referring to a long stretch of climbing without protection

Screamers (Yates Screamers): load-limiting quickdraws that are sewn in such a manner as to lessen the impact of a fall on protection or anchors

second: the second person on a rope team, usually also the leader's belayer

self-arrest: a method of stopping a fall on steep snow or low angle ice

sling or runner: a webbing loop used for a variety of purposes to anchor to the rock

smear: to stand on the front of the foot and gain friction against the rock across the breadth of the sole to adhere to the rock

stance: a standing rest spot, often the sight of the belay

stem: to bridge between two widely-spaced holds

Supergaiters: gaiters that enclose the entire boot

tyrolean traverse: a means of crossing a gap between rock formations via a rope strung between them

thin: a climb or hold of relatively featureless character

toprope: a belay from an anchor point above; protects the climber from falling even a short distance

traverse: to move sideways, without altitude gain

verglas: extremely thin ice plastered to rock

wall or big wall: a long climb traditionally done over multiple days, but may take just a few hours for ace climbers

COPYRIGHTS AND PERMISSIONS

"The Shroud Solo" © copyright by Ivan Ghirardini. Originally published in *La Montagne*, 1976.

"The Desire: A Solo Ascent of the Dihedral Wall" © copyright by Jim Beyer. Originally published in *Climbing* magazine, #41, March/April 1977.

"Party of One: Profile of Jim Beyer, an American Soloist" © copyright 1993 by Greg Child. Reprinted with permission of the publisher from *Mixed Emotions: Mountaineering Writings of Greg Child*, published by The Mountaineers, Seattle, WA.

"The First Solo Ascent of Mount Everest" Original German copyright © R. Piper GmbH & Co. KG, Munchen, 1989. English translation © Hodder & Stoughton 1991. Reprinted with permission of the North American publisher from *Free Spirit: A Climber's Life* by Reinhold Messner, published by The Mountaineers, Seattle, WA.

"Fool's Goal: Shawangunk Solo Climbs" © copyright by Russ Clune. Originally published in *Climbing* magazine, #95, April 1986.

"Kumbhakarna—My Way" © copyright by Tomo Cesen. Originally published in the *American Alpine Journal*, #64, Volume 32, 1990.

"The Only Blasphemy" © copyright by John Long. From *Gorilla Monsoon*, Chockstone Press, 1989.

"Our Man in Everest: Maurice Wilson Surfaces Every Few Years, Only to Be Dutifully Reburied" © copyright by Lawrence Millman. From *Summit* magazine, Volume 38, #4, Winter 1992-1993.

The Adventure Series

The charter statement for the Falcon Adventure Series is ambitious: leave no stone unturned in the search for those rare and timeless stories of legendary achievements. Collected and edited by climber and adventurer John Long, each collection of gripping stories will keep both the adrenaline-driven participant and the armchair adventure riveted.

The Big Drop
Classic Big Wave
Surfing Stories

The Liquid Locomotive
Legendary Whitewater
River Stories

...and more adventure books to come

Close Calls recounts 68 true tales of climbers who let down their guard and lived to tell about it. Written in classic John Long style with a potent combination of levity and sobriety, and accompanied by Tami Knight's wickedly hilarious cartoons, this book is equal parts entertainment and instruction.

Also available the **How to Rock Climb!** series which includes the most complete guide on rock climbing technique and more than 80 guides on where-to-go for prime rock climbing experiences.